Checkers

WEDDING

Checklists,
tips, and step-by-step
preparations

by Annette Spence

A FIRESIDE BOOK
Published by Simon & Schuster Inc.
New York London Toronto Sydney Tokyo Singapore

A TERN BOOK
Copyright © 1985 by Tern Enterprises

First Fireside Edition, 1987
Simon & Schuster Inc.
Rockefeller Center
1230 Avenue of the Americas
New York, New York 10020

Originally published by Blueberry Books

FIRESIDE and colophon are registered
trademarks of Simon & Schuster Inc.

ISBN 0-671-63506-9

CHECKERS: YOUR WEDDING
was prepared and produced by
Tern Enterprise, Inc.
15 West 26th Street
New York, New York 10010

Editor: Mary Forsell
Designer: Lesley Achitoff

Typeset by Paragraphics
Cover color separations by Hong Kong Scanner Craft Company Ltd.
Printed and bound in Hong Kong by Leefung-Asco Printers Ltd.

5 7 9 10 8 6

Contents

How to Use This Book

An innovation among self-help books, CHECKERS help you organize a part of your life, whether it's guiding you through a new situation or helping you complete a project efficiently. By gathering the facts and ordering the chores ahead of time, you can easily attend to even the most complex chore.

Each CHECKERS checklist is self-contained; it provides you with the necessary information to carry out one task or a series of related tasks. As a whole, the volume organizes and simplifies the event—whether it is moving to a new city, planning a wedding, or preparing for the arrival of a new baby.

The checklists, or checkers, also serve as reminders; they outline the course of action and spell out all the niggling details you might not think of but need to know. Some of the checkers bring special points to your attention; these are highlighted in red and most are keyed to a helpful hint that appears at the end of the checklist. Many of the checkers also provide ample room for you to write your own notes to supplement our lists.

For added usefulness, the pages of these volumes can easily be torn from the spiral binding, making it simple to take a list with you shopping or on a comparison trip. Or you can fill out the checklists, leaving only the ones that complete the event (such as when you're comparing caterers for a wedding).

With CHECKERS in hand, you can do away with last-minute rushing and worry. These CHECKERS are designed to make life a little easier for you and a lot more pleasant for everyone involved. Use these lists and you'll feel that you've really accomplished something.

1
First Things First

Congratulations! You've just made what is believed to be the biggest decision of your life. You may feel as if you would just like to sit back and bask in the prewedding limelight, or perhaps you want to rush ahead with wedding preparation. One thing is certain. The minute you utter ''engagement,'' the instant you flash a ring, the second they hear the news, everyone wants to know: Have you set the date? Before you know it, you'll have your wedding party lined up, the perfect reception in order, and your guests bidding you good luck. The ball is rolling now, and you dive headfirst into weeks, *months* of planning.

That's what this first section is all about. Here are the checkers that will help you get your decisions and plans in order. Before you brief the flower girl's mother on rehearsal time, before you begin packing for a Caribbean cruise, better dial a few numbers, ask a few questions, check off a few lists. First things first!

Take a look now at the first of your checkers; they're organized for you and for various members of the wedding party. First you'll consult the master checker for the entire process: a separate PLANNING SCHEDULE for the BRIDE and GROOM. Here are checkers to plan your every move from the moment you announce your engagement (six months or earlier) to one week before the wedding. As much as you may enjoy making decisions, as organized as you may be, everyone knows that two heads are better than one. Make sure the groom receives the PLANNING SCHEDULE right away, and then put your heads together to concoct the best of weddings.

Next is SETTING A BUDGET. You can't plan too far ahead without knowing how much money you will have to spend. Before you deal with real numbers, though, consult the traditional GUIDELINES. In a nutshell, the bride's parents take on most of the wedding expenses while the groom and his family handle the rehearsal dinner and honeymoon. However, feel free to improvise. Do not be limited by rules that seem unreasonable or are unrealistic for your particular situation. Then you must tackle the actual figures with the ESTI-MATES checklist. In order to arrive at a rounded-off figure to aim for, you simply break down the ingredients. This checker does that for you; all you do is come up with the numbers.

The WEDDING & RECEPTION SITES checklist is not designed to slot you at the Waldorf for November 30 but to give you some novel ideas about types of ceremonies and receptions you can have. It also gives you a few tips on what to consider while you're deciding.

THE CEREMONY is more to the point. Since you'll probably have to meet with THE OFFICIANT early in the planning stages, there are a number of questions you should ask. This list gives you an idea of what to keep in mind. Then there's the little matter of VOWS and PERSONALIZING in your ceremony. Many couples are taking a second look at the traditional vows; some are rewriting them; others are altering them just a little; and still others are adding their own unique touches throughout. Here's a step-by-step rundown of where you might rewrite, alter, or add to your ceremony, plus a few new ideas.

Maybe you already know who you want to include in THE WEDDING PARTY or maybe you're in a dilemma. Follow your heart. If you know that your best friend's going to be supportive all the way, then choose her as your maid of honor. Have your groom select his attendants too, and then enter everyone on your list.

Next on the agenda: The best man is at a total loss as to the obligations of his new title. No problem! The duties are spelled out for the MAID OF HONOR, BEST MAN, GROOMSMEN and USHERS in this section. Tear them out, copy extras for you and the different ushers, and distribute them.

√ *Planning Schedule:* √
Bride

First
☐ Tell your family and friends about the engagement.
☐ Discuss wedding specifics with fiancé and your parents.

Six Months Before
☐ Decide how many guests to invite; tell parents.
☐ Choose attendants.
☐ Choose women's wedding attire and accessories.
☐ Select florist and discuss your ideas.
☐ Choose caterer or make arrangements for reception food.
☐ Select china, crystal, and silver. Register in a wedding gift registry.
☐ Discuss honeymoon plans with fiancé.
☐ Visit clergymember with fiancé.
☐ Book ceremony and reception sites.
☐ Decide what kind of reception music you want. If necessary, begin interviewing musicians.

Three Months Before
☐ Set up appointment for blood test and examination.
☐ Complete guest list.
☐ Order stationery.
☐ Choose rings with fiancé.
☐ Confer reception details with professionals.
☐ Interview and select a photographer.

One Month Before
☐ Choose bridesmaids' and groom's gifts.
☐ Order wedding cake.
☐ Begin writing thank-you notes for gifts received.
☐ Discuss rehearsal party arrangements with host.

- ☐ Arrange bridesmaids' luncheon or party.
- ☐ Arrange lodging for out-of-town bridesmaids.
- ☐ Apply for marriage license with fiancé.
- ☐ Arrange wedding transportation.
- ☐ Schedule final fittings for the women's wedding attire, including your own. Check on delivery dates.
- ☐ Prepare for, schedule, and have formal portraits taken.
- ☐ Send wedding announcements and photos to papers.

Two Weeks Before

- ☐ Change your name and address on legal documents.
- ☐ Confirm details with florist, photographer, caterer, musicians, etc.
- ☐ Schedule rehearsal for one or two days before.

One Week Before

- ☐ Begin honeymoon packing.
- ☐ Set aside your wedding attire.
- ☐ Address and stamp wedding announcements to mail immediately after the reception.
- ☐ Wrap your bridesmaids' gifts for presentation at the luncheon or rehearsal dinner.
- ☐ Attend (or give) the bridesmaids' luncheon.
- ☐ Brief everyone on the rehearsal time.

Notes

First

☐ Tell your family and friends about the engagement.

☐ Discuss wedding specifics with fiancée and your parents.

☐ Decide how (and if) you'll split expenses.

Six Months Before

☐ Help fiancée decide on the guest list number.

☐ Start your own list; have your family do the same.

☐ Select best man and groomsmen.

☐ Help fiancée with general planning (florist, caterer, sites, etc.).

☐ Discuss and decide honeymoon plans; begin making arrangements.

☐ Visit clergymember with fiancée.

Three Months Before

☐ Complete guest list.

☐ Help select and order stationery.

☐ Select the men's attire with fiancée; consult attendants, then ask for sizes and arrange a fitting. Order your own wedding attire.

☐ Choose rings with your fiancée.

☐ Set up appointments for blood test and examination.

One Month Before

☐ Help fiancée finish mailing invitations.

☐ Talk to fiancée about her bouquet and going-away corsage. Order the bride's flowers along with the mothers' corsages and the men's boutonnieres.

☐ Choose attendants' and bride's gifts.

☐ Begin writing thank-you notes for gifts.

☐ Make arrangements for rehearsal dinner with your

parents (or whoever is hosting it).

- ☐ Arrange the bachelor's party, if you're hosting.
- ☐ Arrange lodging for out-of-town attendants.
- ☐ Apply for marriage license with your fiancée.
- ☐ Pick up rings.
- ☐ Help arrange wedding transportation.
- ☐ Make sure the men's wedding attire has been ordered, fitted, and that delivery date is set.

Two Weeks Before

- ☐ Check all policies, deeds, and records, and make any necessary changes.
- ☐ Confirm details with all wedding consultants.
- ☐ Confirm honeymoon plans.
- ☐ Get a haircut.

One Week Before

- ☐ Begin your honeymoon packing.
- ☐ Pick up wedding attire at least two days ahead to correct any unforeseen problems.
- ☐ Wrap your attendants' gifts for presentation at rehearsal dinner or bachelor's party.
- ☐ Brief attendants on rehearsal time.
- ☐ Explain special seating arrangement to best man.
- ☐ Give the clergymember's fee in sealed envelope to best man, who will present it just before or after the ceremony.

Notes

Before you make too many wedding plans, you should divide expenses and finalize the amount of money you're able to spend.

☐ Sit down with both sets of parents and discuss your ideas.

☐ Traditionally, the bride's parents handle all wedding costs while the groom's parents take care of the rehearsal dinner.

☐ However, the rules are more flexible now. The groom's parents may share expenses, or you and the groom may finance the wedding yourselves.

Here is the traditional breakdown. Extra lines allow you to make alterations.

The Bride and/or Her Family

☐ Invitations   ☐ Engagement party   ☐ Attendants' party   ☐ Gifts: groom, maids   ☐ Groom's ring
☐ Medical exam, blood test   ☐ Lodging for out-of-town maids   ☐ Wedding dress, veil, accessories
☐ Flowers: ceremony, reception   ☐ Flowers: maids, flower girls   ☐ Photographs: engagement, wedding   ☐ Musicians, entertainment   ☐ Rental fees: church, equipment   ☐ Wedding gift book, guest book   ☐ Transportation for wedding party to reception   ☐ All reception costs   ☐ Thank-you notes

☐ _____   ☐ _____

☐ _____   ☐ _____

☐ _____   ☐ _____

The Groom and/or His Family

☐ Bride's engagement and wedding rings   ☐ Marriage license   ☐ Medical exam, blood test   ☐ Gifts: bride, attendants   ☐ Rehearsal dinner   ☐ Groom's attire   ☐ Lodging for out-of-town attendants
☐ Clergymember's fee   ☐ Flowers: bride, mothers, special guests   ☐ Boutonnieres: groom, attendants, fathers   ☐ Honeymoon

☐ _____   ☐ _____

☐ _____   ☐ _____

☐ _____   ☐ _____

☐ _____   ☐ _____

Attendants

☐ Transportation to wedding location   ☐ Gift for the couple   ☐ Own wedding attire   ☐ Parties for the couple (shower, bachelor's party)

Helpful Hints

- If your groom's parents will be helping you with the costs, send them the bill for specific expenses, rather than asking for a percentage of the total cost.

- Some expenses are optional or set by local custom: The bride and groom may pay for attendants' attire: relatives or friends may host the rehearsal dinner; the groom may give his own bachelor's party; and the bride may buy her mother's and grandmothers' corsages.

Notes

Setting a Budget:
Estimates

A little research—a few quick phone calls to a local photographer, dress shop, and the engravers, plus advice from consultants and newlywed friends—will help you keep your expenses in perspective, as well as to aim at an overall cost.

☐ **Stationery**   ☐ **Total** $_____
- ☐ Invitations $_____ ☐ Announcements $_____
- ☐ Thank-you notes $_____ ☐ Matches $_____
- ☐ Napkins $_____ ☐ _____ $_____
- ☐ _____ $_____ ☐ _____ $_____

☐ **Parties**   ☐ **Total** $_____
- ☐ Engagement $_____ ☐ Maids' $_____
- ☐ Bachelor's $_____ ☐ Rehearsal $_____

☐ **Flowers**   ☐ **Total** $_____
- ☐ Bride's $_____ ☐ Maids' $_____
- ☐ Mothers' $_____ ☐ Special guests $_____
- ☐ Groom's $_____ ☐ Ushers' $_____
- ☐ Ceremony site $_____
- ☐ Reception site $_____
- ☐ _____ $_____ ☐ _____ $_____

☐ **Women's Wedding Attire**   ☐ **Total** $_____
- ☐ Bride's dress $_____
- ☐ Headpiece, veil $_____
- ☐ Accessories $_____ ☐ _____ $_____

☐ **Men's Wedding Attire**   ☐ **Total** $_____
- ☐ Groom's formal wear $_____
- ☐ Accessories: $_____ ☐ _____ $_____

13

☐ **Gifts**   ☐ **Total** $_____
   ☐ Bride's $_____ ☐ Groom's $_____
   ☐ Rings $_____ ☐ Maids' $_____
   ☐ Ushers' $_____ ☐ _____ $_____

☐ **Fees**   ☐ **Total** $_____
   ☐ Ceremony site rental $_____
   ☐ Reception site rental $_____
   ☐ Equipment rental $_____
   ☐ Officiant $_____
   ☐ Medical $_____ ☐ _____ $_____

☐ **Photography**   ☐ **Total** _____
   ☐ Formal portraits: engagement $_____
   ☐ Formal portraits: wedding $_____
   ☐ Candids $_____ ☐ Extras $_____

☐ **Food**   ☐ **Total** $_____
   ☐ Cake $_____ ☐ Liquor $_____
   ☐ _____ $_____ ☐ _____ $_____

☐ **Music**   ☐ **Total** $_____
   ☐ Wedding $_____ ☐ Reception $_____

☐ **Transportation**   ☐ **Total** $_____
   ☐ Limousines $_____ ☐ _____ $_____

☐ **Special Services**   ☐ **Total** $_____
   ☐ _____ $_____ ☐ _____ $_____
☐ **Grand Total** $_____

Notes

✓ *Wedding & Reception Sites* ✓

Book your ceremony and reception site *at least* six months before the wedding date—nine months or more in a big city or in the popular wedding months of June, August, September, and December.

Find your ideal wedding site by answering these questions:

☐ Will the ceremony be religious or civil? Of course, this depends on how big a role religion plays in your life.

☐ Who will officiate? Your childhood minister at your own church or the Justice of the Peace in a local courthouse?

☐ Will it fit your guest list? Don't try to cram 300 well-wishers in your parent's living room.

☐ Have you considered special settings? A military wedding in your academy chapel? The deck of a yacht? The botanical gardens?

Before you select your reception site, you may want to consider one that offers a package deal, such as many clubs and reception halls do.

☐ Rental estimate _____ includes:

☐ Food? ☐ Beverages? ☐ Wedding cake?

☐ Entertainment? ☐ Equipment (chairs, tables, etc.)

☐ Waiters, waitresses? ☐ Bartenders?

☐ Parking valets?

Now, see if you have coordinated your wedding and reception sites.

☐ Ceremony location _____

☐ Reception location _____

☐ Ceremony time _____ ☐ Reception time _____
Reception style:
☐ Buffet ☐ Sit-down ☐ Brunch ☐ Cake and punch ☐ Cocktails/hors d'oeuvre
☐ Other _____

Helpful Hints

- If you plan to hold the reception at your ceremony site (say, in the basement of your church), consider whether any building restrictions or behavior codes fit in with your party plans.

Notes

The Ceremony:
Officiant

Once you've decided who you would like to pronounce you husband and wife, you have many questions to ask him/her. You and your groom should schedule an appointment as soon as possible.

☐ Name _____ ☐ Phone _____
☐ Address _____ ☐ Date _____

Questions:

☐ What restrictions should we be aware of?
   ☐ Former divorce?
   ☐ Different faiths?
   ☐ Nonchurch member?
   ☐ Age
   ☐ Other _____

☐ Could we have a copy of the traditional ceremony, and any newer services with modified wording?

☐ Are we permitted to rewrite our vows?

☐ What parts of the traditional vows may not be changed?

☐ Are we required to attend counseling classes before we can be married by you (or in your church)?

☐ Will you marry us in a nontraditional setting?

☐ Will we be permitted to carry out our wedding plans in your church (candles, extra chairs, photography, live or recorded music, dress, etc.)?

☐ What services can your church provide (organist, reception facilities)?

☐ Can we make an appointment with you for the rehearsal? _____

☐ What is your fee? _____

☐ What does it include?
   ☐ Church   ☐ Organist?   ☐ Custodial services?

☐ Other _____

☐ More questions: _____

_____

_____

_____

_____

Helpful Hints

- A bride and groom of different faiths may marry in a ceremony that combines both services. Consult your clergymember for ideas and permission. You may, for example, alternate the religious readings and combine the vows; or have the clergymember of one faith perform the entire ceremony, then let the other give a short blessing at the end.

Notes

The Ceremony:
✓Vows & Personalizing✓

Your wedding vows don't have to be strictly by the book; you may wish to change a little or a lot of the ceremony. Consult your clergy-member (See "The Ceremony: Officiator") for the denomination's requirements. Then:

☐ Study the vows and symbolism. What do you like and dislike?

_____

_____

_____

_____

_____

☐ Gather more information. Research libraries for books on current wedding innovations, poems, prayers, and hymns.

Sources: _____

_____

_____

_____

_____

☐ You might want to include other people in your ceremony, too, for special readings or performances—all for a "personal touch" in your wedding. **Where do they belong? Here is the natural order of the ceremony.**

☐ Procession _____

☐ Welcome _____

☐ Giving away _____

☐ Prayer/Reading _____

☐ Groom's vows _____

☐ Bride's vows _____

- ☐ Prayer/Reading   _____
- ☐ Blessing the rings   _____
- ☐ Exchanging the rings   _____
- ☐ Prayer/Reading   _____
- ☐ Pronouncement   _____
- ☐ Kiss/Closing   _____
- ☐ Recession   _____

Helpful Hints

More "Personal" Ideas

- Have *both* your parents, one on each arm, escort you to the altar.

- Include children from a previous marriage in the wedding.

- Greet your guests at the entrance as they arrive.

√ *The Wedding Party* √

You and your groom choose your own attendants, ideally, about six months before the wedding. Who's in the running? Cherished relatives and dear friends.

1. Formal: Choose four to twelve attendants (one usher for every fifty guests).
2. Semiformal: Select two to six attendants each.
3. Informal: Limit your choices to one honor attendant and *maybe* one extra maid or groomsman.

☐ Maid of honor _____
   Phone _____ Address _____
   _____

☐ Bridesmaid _____
   Phone _____ Address _____
   _____

☐ Bridesmaid _____
   Phone _____ Address _____
   _____

☐ Bridesmaid _____
   Phone _____ Address _____
   _____

☐ Bridesmaid _____
   Phone _____ Address _____
   _____

☐ Flower girl _____
   Phone _____ Address _____
   _____

☐ Ringbearer _____
   Phone _____ Address _____
   _____

☐ Trainbearer _____

    Phone _____ Address _____

    _____

☐ Best man _____

    Phone _____ Address _____

    _____

☐ Groomsman _____

    Phone _____ Address _____

    _____

☐ Groomsman _____

    Phone _____ Address _____

    _____

☐ Groomsman _____

    Phone _____ Address _____

    _____

☐ Groomsman _____

    Phone _____ Address _____

    _____

Helpful Hints

- Child attendants (flower girl, ringbearer, trainbearer) are usually between the ages of four and eight.

- Children should attend rehearsal to practice their parts, but they are not required to attend prewedding parties, although the adult attendants should.

- If you can't include all your friends in the wedding party, ask them to take charge of the guest book, give out wedding programs, serve punch, etc.

√ *Maid of Honor* √

What are the official duties of the maid or matron of honor, and how can you really help the bride? Your chief responsibilities are as follows:

☐ Assemble and pay for your wedding attire.
☐ Attend all prewedding parties in the couple's honor.
☐ Sign the marriage license.
☐ Arrive early at the bride's house before the wedding to help her dress.
☐ Keep track of the time, and see that the other atttendants arrive promptly at the wedding.
☐ Precede the bride and her father in the procession.
☐ Arrange the bride's train and veil during the ceremony, and hold the groom's ring.
☐ Stand next to the groom in the receiving line and sit on his left at the bride's table.
☐ Help the bride change into her traveling clothes before she leaves for the honeymoon.
☐ Most important: Give the bride all the support she needs, whether it be emotional or physical.

Now, for the support that isn't necessarily one of your responsibilities, but will certainly earn the bride's gratitude:

☐ Take charge of recording and displaying the gifts.
☐ Arrange to have the bridesmaids fitted, and make sure their dresses are in perfect condition for the wedding.
☐ Offer to babysit younger brothers and sisters while the bride and her mother run wedding errands.
☐ Help the bride select her wedding attire and other items of her trousseau.

☐ Return rented equipment and formal wear while the couple are on their honeymoon.
☐ Pick up any last-minute items.
☐ Suggest that the bridesmaids help with the wedding preparations.
☐ Sneak the bride away from the commotion of planning in the final weeks for a movie, dinner, or shopping.

☐ Wedding date _____ ☐ Time _____
☐ Fittings _____
☐ Shower _____
_____

Notes

 Best Man

Sure, you're honored to be your buddy's best man, but now what? Here's what is customarily expected of you:

- ☐ Assemble and pay for your own wedding attire.
- ☐ Sign the marriage license.
- ☐ See that the groom is dressed properly before the wedding.
- ☐ Make sure that you have a check available for the clergymember's fee. (Give it to him just before or after the ceremony.)
- ☐ Enter the vestibule immediately after the groom during the procession. Then stand behind the groom, slightly to the left.
- ☐ Hold the bride's ring until the officiant asks for it.
- ☐ Walk out with the maid of honor after the ceremony. (Or you may leave through a side door while the recession goes down the aisle, according to the couple's wishes.)
- ☐ Help the bride and groom into their car once the ceremony is over.
- ☐ Drive the couple to the reception (unless there is a hired driver).
- ☐ Mingle with the guests at the reception.
- ☐ Propose the first toast to the new couple.
- ☐ See that the reception flows smoothly—without the practical jokes.
- ☐ Help the groom get into his going-away clothes.
- ☐ Assist with the groom's last-minute packing.
- ☐ Take charge of the honeymoon luggage.
- ☐ Escort the couple to the exit and to the car. (You may even take them to the airport.)

- [ ] Handle keys, tickets, and other small details until just before the couple leave for the honeymoon.
- [ ] See that the men's rented clothing is returned in good condition.

- [ ] Wedding date _____ [ ] Time_____
- [ ] Fittings _____
- [ ] Bachelor's party _____

Notes

You may be a groomsman, and usher, or both; the distinction is actually self-explanatory. It's just that some weddings are larger and require different people to fill both roles, while in other weddings, the groomsmen escort guests in, and then join the groom and best man in the vestibule.

Groomsmen

☐ Assemble and pay for your own wedding outfit.

☐ Escort guests to their seats (optional).

☐ Participate in the procession and recession.

☐ Direct guests to parking, restroom facilities, and the reception site.

☐ Propose toasts during the reception.

☐ Mingle among the guests and dance with the single women. (Why? To keep the party alive!)

Ushers

☐ Be at the ceremony site 45 minutes to an hour before the wedding.

☐ Line up on the left side of the entrance.

☐ As guests arrive, step forward and offer your right arm to each female.

☐ Escort bride's friends and relatives to seats at the left side of the aisle, groom's guests to the right.

☐ When a man and woman arrive together, take the woman's arm and let the man follow a step or two steps behind.

☐ When several women arrive together, escort the eldest first while the others follow.

☐ Simply escort (without the arm) single men to their seats.

- ☐ Make polite small talk with the guests as you're escorting.
- ☐ See the best man about any special seating arrangements (honored or handicapped guests).

- ☐ Wedding date _____ ☐ Time _____
- ☐ Fittings _____
- ☐ Bachelor's party _____

Notes

2
Putting Together the Reception

This is the section for shoppers: Prices and quality vary, and it's well worth your while to look around before you book your reception professionals.

That's why we can't stress this enough to you: Begin early. A planning period of six months is ideal, but if you allow more time, you're bound to do even better.

Start by relying on our hints for COMPARISON SHOPPING and CONTRACTS. They'll guide you as you interview each professional, sample each dish and outline each contract. After all, you want everything to meet your specifications exactly and perfectly. Here, you're advised on how to set the rules in motion, pinpoint your needs, and get agreements in writing. When it comes to your wedding reception, why settle for good when you can make it *great*—even on a modest budget.

Next are the ESTIMATES—three of each for the CATERER, BAKER, FLORIST, MUSICIANS & ENTERTAINMENT, and PHOTOGRAPHER. These checkers help you carefully outline, select, and budget the items you'll need for each category. Your preferences determine how much attention you want to give and how much money you want to allot to each category; for example, you may want to have a lavish food spread but a minimum of photography; or maybe not so much music as flowers. Using these checkers is an easy way to make sure you're keeping within the budget you drew up in earlier checklists, as well as a means of ensuring that you have considered all of the elements that are so vital to the reception. This is how to do it: Take a checklist along with you when you see each professional. Ask questions, look at samples, make notes, and get your estimates. Try to see three different professionals for each category. Later you'll compare your notes, select the professional you'd like to work with, and tear out the other two estimates.

Also included is helpful information—such as how long before the wedding you should place your order, how to make payments wisely, and much more—that will simplify coordinating your reception. You'll find that these checklists will help you keep things in order and will also stimulate your imagination so that you can create a sumptuous symphony of food, music, flowers, and memories. You have your resources here, so get started!

✓ *Comparison Shopping* ✓
& Contracts

Before you book your various consultants and services, consult the shopping guidelines below. *Always* make sure all your receipts, agreements, and contracts are in order.

☐ Begin early. You'll notice that this checker suggests you shop months in advance, and with good reason. This way, you'll be able to examine your options and costs, and make decisions at your leisure.

☐ Collect references. Ask newlywed friends about their good and bad experiences: a caterer with an outstanding display or photographer who ''steals the show.'' Maybe Dad or Aunt Nancy has a good friend in the florist business who'll do you right.

☐ Get estimates. You can either approach a consultant with your specific plans, or call anonymously. Never be too shy to ask for a discount, especially if you'll be purchasing a large volume.

☐ Make your budget limitations clear. If you know you can't overspend, you might as well as stop the bandleader the minute he quotes you a sky-high fee.

☐ Check for quality. Ask to see equipment, photos, samples, and whatever will be proof of a consultant's or professional's performance. Check with the Better Business Bureau to see if a company has any records of complaints.

☐ Get contracts or agreements in writing. Spell out the details: cost, time, place, and descriptions of the ambience you'd like to create. Study contract before you sign and add last-minute notes in pen.

☐ Be cautious with payments. You'll be required to put down a deposit on most services or goods, but don't pay in full until everything has been delivered to your satisfaction. Use credit cards whenever you can; you'll always have proof of payment. If you do write a check, don't make it out to ''cash,'' but to the company or individual.

☐ Know what to do upon cancellation. In most cases, you'll lose your deposit. You may be liable for some costs of the full contract, too; it varies from state to state. Check with your state's Attorney General office about what the percentage or ceiling is. It's a good idea to get that percentage in writing on your contract before you sign.

Notes

Estimates:
Caterer

Begin interviewing prospective caterers about six months before the wedding. By three months before, you should be confirming details with whomever you've chosen. Everything should be in order by two weeks before.

☐ **Name** _____ ☐ **Phone** _____

☐ **Food**	No.	Cost per	Total
☐ Hors d'oeuvre	___	___	___
☐ Main course	___	___	___
☐ Dessert	___	___	___
☐ Other____	___	___	___
_____	___	___	___
☐ **Beverages**			
☐ Alcoholic	___	___	___
☐ Liquor	___	___	___
☐ Champagne	___	___	___
☐ Wine	___	___	___
☐ _____	___	___	___
☐ Nonalcoholic	___	___	___
☐ Punch	___	___	___
☐ _____	___	___	___
☐ **Services**			
☐ Waiters	___	___	___
☐ Bartenders	___	___	___
☐ Parking valet	___	___	___
☐ _____	___	___	___
☐ _____	___	___	___
☐ **Equipment**			
☐ Tables	___	___	___
☐ Chairs	___	___	___

☐ Linens   _____ _____ _____
☐ _____   _____ _____ _____
☐ _____   _____ _____ _____

☐ **Total estimate $**_____
☐ **Actual cost $**_____
☐ **Deposit $**_____
☐ **Balance due $**_____
☐ **Caterer's arrival time** _____

Notes

Estimates:

Caterer

Begin interviewing prospective caterers about six months before the wedding. By three months before, you should be confirming details with whomever you've chosen. Everything should be in order by two weeks before.

☐ **Name** _____ ☐ **Phone** _____

☐ **Food**	**No.**	**Cost per**	**Total**
☐ Hors d'oeuvre	___	___	___
☐ Main course	___	___	___
☐ Dessert	___	___	___
☐ Other____	___	___	___
	___	___	___
☐ **Beverages**			
☐ Alcoholic			
☐ Liquor	___	___	___
☐ Champagne	___	___	___
☐ Wine	___	___	___
☐ ____	___	___	___
☐ Nonalcoholic	___	___	___
☐ Punch	___	___	___
☐ ____	___	___	___
☐ **Services**			
☐ Waiters	___	___	___
☐ Bartenders	___	___	___
☐ Parking valet	___	___	___
☐ ____	___	___	___
☐ ____	___	___	___
☐ **Equipment**			
☐ Tables	___	___	___
☐ Chairs	___	___	___

☐ Linens   _____ _____ _____

☐ _____   _____ _____ _____

☐ _____   _____ _____ _____

☐ **Total estimate $**_____

☐ **Actual cost $**_____

☐ **Deposit $**_____

☐ **Balance due $**_____

☐ **Caterer's arrival time** _____

Notes

Estimates:
√*Caterer* √

Begin interviewing prospective caterers about six months before the wedding. By three months before, you should be confirming details with whomever you've chosen. Everything should be in order by two weeks before.

☐ **Name** _____	☐ **Phone**_____		
☐ **Food**	**No.**	**Cost per**	**Total**
☐ Hors d'oeuvre	___	___	___
☐ Main course	___	___	___
☐ Dessert	___	___	___
☐ Other_____	___	___	___
_____	___	___	___
☐ **Beverages**			
☐ Alcoholic	___	___	___
☐ Liquor	___	___	___
☐ Champagne	___	___	___
☐ Wine	___	___	___
☐ _____	___	___	___
☐ Nonalcoholic	___	___	___
☐ Punch	___	___	___
☐ _____	___	___	___
☐ **Services**			
☐ Waiters	___	___	___
☐ Bartenders	___	___	___
☐ Parking valet	___	___	___
☐ _____	___	___	___
☐ _____	___	___	___
☐ **Equipment**			
☐ Tables	___	___	___
☐ Chairs	___	___	___

☐ Linens   _____ _____ _____

☐ _____   _____ _____ _____

☐ _____   _____ _____ _____

☐ **Total estimate $**_____

☐ **Actual cost $**_____

☐ **Deposit $**_____

☐ **Balance due $**_____

☐ **Caterer's arrival time** _____

Notes

Estimates:
Baker

You should order your cake (and additional pastries, groom's cake, etc.) one month before, but you might enjoy shopping and sampling as early as two months before. Take this checklist along for a little help, but remember: The possibilities are endless!

☐ **Shop** _____ ☐ **Phone** _____

Wedding Cake

☐ For how many guests? _____

☐ **Shape**
   ☐ Round ☐ Square ☐ Triangular
   ☐ Heart ☐ Rings ☐ Other _____

☐ **Tiers**
   ☐ One ☐ Two ☐ Three
   ☐ Four ☐ Other _____

☐ **Cake flavor**
   ☐ White ☐ Yellow ☐ Chocolate
   ☐ Lemon ☐ Spice ☐ Carrot
   ☐ Pound ☐ Other _____

☐ **Filling flavor**
   ☐ Strawberry ☐ Chocolate ☐ Lemon
   ☐ Fruit ☐ Coconut ☐ Mousse
   ☐ Other _____

☐ **Icing flavor/color**
   ☐ Vanilla ☐ Chocolate ☐ Buttercream
   ☐ German chocolate ☐ Other _____

☐ **Decorations**
   ☐ Bride and groom ☐ Flowers
   ☐ Lovebirds ☐ Bells ☐ Rings

☐ Other _____
☐ Specifics _____
_____
_____
_____

Groom's Cake
☐ **Variations**
   ☐ Top wedding cake layer
   ☐ Packaged for guests   ☐ Separate cake

☐ **Flavors**
   ☐ Chocolate   ☐ Pound
   ☐ Fruitcake   ☐ Other _____

☐ Specifics _____
_____
_____

Extras
   ☐ Packaged cakes   ☐ Pastries
   ☐ _____   ☐ _____

Estimates
☐ Wedding cake	$	_____
☐ Groom's cake	$	_____
☐ _____	$	_____
☐ _____	$	_____
Total	**$**	_____

☐ **Actual cost $_____**   ☐ **Deposit $_____**
☐ **Balance due $_____**
☐ **Cake arrival time _____**

Estimates: Baker

You should order your cake (and additional pastries, groom's cake, etc.) one month before, but you might enjoy shopping and sampling as early as two months before. Take this checklist along for a little help, but remember: The possibilities are endless!

☐ **Shop** _____ ☐ **Phone** _____

Wedding Cake

☐ For how many guests? _____

☐ **Shape**
  ☐ Round ☐ Square ☐ Triangular
  ☐ Heart ☐ Rings ☐ Other _____

☐ **Tiers**
  ☐ One ☐ Two ☐ Three
  ☐ Four ☐ Other _____

☐ **Cake flavor**
  ☐ White ☐ Yellow ☐ Chocolate
  ☐ Lemon ☐ Spice ☐ Carrot
  ☐ Pound ☐ Other _____

☐ **Filling flavor**
  ☐ Strawberry ☐ Chocolate ☐ Lemon
  ☐ Fruit ☐ Coconut ☐ Mousse
  ☐ Other _____

☐ **Icing flavor/color**
  ☐ Vanilla ☐ Chocolate ☐ Buttercream
  ☐ German chocolate ☐ Other _____

☐ **Decorations**
  ☐ Bride and groom ☐ Flowers
  ☐ Lovebirds ☐ Bells ☐ Rings

☐ Other _____
☐ Specifics _____
_____
_____
_____

Groom's Cake
☐ Variations
  ☐ Top wedding cake layer
  ☐ Packaged for guests   ☐ Separate cake

☐ Flavors
  ☐ Chocolate   ☐ Pound
  ☐ Fruitcake   ☐ Other _____

☐ Specifics _____
_____
_____

Extras
  ☐ Packaged cakes   ☐ Pastries
  ☐ _____   ☐ _____

Estimates
  ☐ Wedding cake $ _____
  ☐ Groom's cake $ _____
  ☐ _____ $ _____
  ☐ _____ $ _____
            Total $ _____

☐ **Actual cost** $_____   ☐ **Deposit** $_____
☐ **Balance due** $_____
☐ **Cake arrival time** _____

Estimates:
Baker

You should order your cake (and additional pastries, groom's cake, etc.) one month before, but you might enjoy shopping and sampling as early as two months before. Take this checklist along for a little help, but remember: The possibilities are endless!

☐ **Shop** _____   ☐ **Phone** _____

Wedding Cake
☐ For how many guests? _____

☐ **Shape**
   ☐ Round   ☐ Square   ☐ Triangular
   ☐ Heart   ☐ Rings   ☐ Other _____

☐ **Tiers**
   ☐ One   ☐ Two   ☐ Three
   ☐ Four   ☐ Other _____

☐ **Cake flavor**
   ☐ White   ☐ Yellow   ☐ Chocolate
   ☐ Lemon   ☐ Spice   ☐ Carrot
   ☐ Pound   ☐ Other _____

☐ **Filling flavor**
   ☐ Strawberry   ☐ Chocolate   ☐ Lemon
   ☐ Fruit   ☐ Coconut   ☐ Mousse
   ☐ Other _____

☐ **Icing flavor/color**
   ☐ Vanilla   ☐ Chocolate   ☐ Buttercream
   ☐ German chocolate   ☐ Other _____

☐ **Decorations**
   ☐ Bride and groom   ☐ Flowers
   ☐ Lovebirds   ☐ Bells   ☐ Rings

☐ Other _____
☐ Specifics _____
_____
_____
_____

Groom's Cake
☐ **Variations**
  ☐ Top wedding cake layer
  ☐ Packaged for guests   ☐ Separate cake

☐ **Flavors**
  ☐ Chocolate   ☐ Pound
  ☐ Fruitcake   ☐ Other _____

☐ Specifics _____
_____
_____

Extras
  ☐ Packaged cakes   ☐ Pastries
  ☐ _____   ☐ _____

  Estimates
  ☐ Wedding cake $ _____
  ☐ Groom's cake $ _____
  ☐ _____ $ _____
  ☐ _____ $ _____
               Total $ _____

☐ **Actual cost $_____**   ☐ **Deposit $_____**
☐ **Balance due $_____**
☐ **Cake arrival time _____**

Estimates: Florist

Select your florist six months or so before your wedding and begin discussing your ideas. Aim for three months before to wrap up details, then check again about two weeks before.

☐ **Name** _____   ☐ **Phone** _____

	Description	Cost

☐ **Bride**
  ☐ Bouquet   _____ _____
  ☐ Headpiece   _____ _____

☐ **Maid of honor**
  ☐ Bouquet   _____ _____
  ☐ Headpiece   _____ _____

☐ **Bridesmaids**
  ☐ Bouquets   _____ _____
  ☐ Headpieces   _____ _____

☐ **Groom**
  ☐ Boutonniere   _____ _____

☐ **Groomsmen**
  ☐ Boutonnieres   _____ _____

☐ **Child attendants**
  ☐ Flower basket   _____ _____
  ☐ Ringbearer's pillow _____ _____
  ☐ Boutonnieres   _____ _____
  ☐ Corsages   _____ _____

☐ **Fathers**
  ☐ Boutonnieres   _____ _____

	Description	Cost
☐ **Mothers**		
☐ Corsages	_____	____
☐ **Special guests**		
☐ Corsages	_____	____
☐ Boutonnieres	_____	____
☐ **Ceremony**		
☐ Altar/canopy	_____	____
☐ Pews	_____	____
☐ Windows	_____	____
☐ Aisles	_____	____
☐ _____	_____	____
☐ _____	_____	____
☐ **Reception**		
☐ Receiving line	_____	____
☐ Tables	_____	____
☐ _____	_____	____
☐ _____	_____	____
☐ _____	_____	____

☐ **Total estimate $** _____

☐ **Actual cost $** _____

☐ **Deposit $** _____

☐ **Arrival time** _____

Notes

Estimates:
Florist

Select your florist six months or so before your wedding and begin discussing your ideas. Aim for three months before to wrap up details, then check again about two weeks before.

☐ **Name** _____ ☐ **Phone** _____

	Description	**Cost**
☐ **Bride**		
☐ Bouquet	_____	_____
☐ Headpiece	_____	_____
☐ **Maid of honor**		
☐ Bouquet	_____	_____
☐ Headpiece	_____	_____
☐ **Bridesmaids**		
☐ Bouquets	_____	_____
☐ Headpieces	_____	_____
☐ **Groom**		
☐ Boutonniere	_____	_____
☐ **Groomsmen**		
☐ Boutonnieres	_____	_____
☐ **Child attendants**		
☐ Flower basket	_____	_____
☐ Ringbearer's pillow	_____	_____
☐ Boutonnieres	_____	_____
☐ Corsages	_____	_____
☐ **Fathers**		
☐ Boutonnieres	_____	_____

	Description	Cost
☐ **Mothers**		
☐ Corsages	_____	____
☐ **Special guests**		
☐ Corsages	_____	____
☐ Boutonnieres	_____	____
☐ **Ceremony**		
☐ Altar/canopy	_____	____
☐ Pews	_____	____
☐ Windows	_____	____
☐ Aisles	_____	____
☐ _____	_____	____
☐ _____	_____	____
☐ **Reception**		
☐ Receiving line	_____	____
☐ Tables	_____	____
☐ _____	_____	____
☐ _____	_____	____
☐ _____	_____	____

☐ **Total estimate $ _____**

☐ **Actual cost $ _____**

☐ **Deposit $ _____**

☐ **Arrival time _____**

Notes

√ Estimates: √
Florist

Select your florist six months or so before your wedding and begin discussing your ideas. Aim for three months before to wrap up details, then check again about two weeks before.

☐ **Name** _____ ☐ **Phone** _____

	Description	**Cost**
☐ **Bride**		
☐ Bouquet	_____	_____
☐ Headpiece	_____	_____
☐ **Maid of honor**		
☐ Bouquet	_____	_____
☐ Headpiece	_____	_____
☐ **Bridesmaids**		
☐ Bouquets	_____	_____
☐ Headpieces	_____	_____
☐ **Groom**		
☐ Boutonniere	_____	_____
☐ **Groomsmen**		
☐ Boutonnieres	_____	_____
☐ **Child attendants**		
☐ Flower basket	_____	_____
☐ Ringbearer's pillow	_____	_____
☐ Boutonnieres	_____	_____
☐ Corsages	_____	_____
☐ **Fathers**		
☐ Boutonnieres	_____	_____

	Description	Cost
☐ **Mothers**		
☐ Corsages	_____	_____
☐ **Special guests**		
☐ Corsages	_____	_____
☐ Boutonnieres	_____	_____
☐ **Ceremony**		
☐ Altar/canopy	_____	_____
☐ Pews	_____	_____
☐ Windows	_____	_____
☐ Aisles	_____	_____
☐ _____	_____	_____
☐ _____	_____	_____
☐ **Reception**		
☐ Receiving line	_____	_____
☐ Tables	_____	_____
☐ _____	_____	_____
☐ _____	_____	_____
☐ _____	_____	_____

☐ **Total estimate $** _____

☐ **Actual cost $** _____

☐ **Deposit $** _____

☐ **Arrival time** _____

Notes

Estimates:
✓ Musicians & Entertainment ✓

If a band or disc jockey is included in your reception plans, begin interviewing—or listening—when you book your reception site, about six months ahead.

☐ **Name(s)** _____   ☐ **Phone** _____

_____   _____

_____   _____

_____   _____

_____   _____

_____   _____

☐ Sound/repertoire _____

_____

_____

_____

☐ Playing time _____
☐ Hours performing _____
☐ Arrival time _____
☐ Attire _____
☐ Special accommodations for equipment _____

_____

_____

☐ Numbers/songs requested
1. _____
2. _____
3. _____
4. _____
5. _____
6. _____
7. _____
8. _____

9. _____

10. _____

☐ **Deposit** $ _____ ☐ **Balance due** $ _____

Notes

If a band or disc jockey is included in your reception plans, begin interviewing—or listening—when you book your reception site, about six months ahead.

☐ **Name(s)** _____   ☐ **Phone** _____

_____   _____

_____   _____

_____   _____

_____   _____

_____   _____

_____   _____

☐ Sound/repertoire _____

_____

_____

_____

☐ Playing time _____
☐ Hours performing _____
☐ Arrival time _____
☐ Attire _____
☐ Special accommodations for equipment _____

_____

_____

☐ Numbers/songs requested
1. _____
2. _____
3. _____
4. _____
5. _____
6. _____
7. _____
8. _____

9. _____
10. _____

☐ **Deposit** $ _____ ☐ **Balance due** $ _____

Notes

Estimates:
✓ Musicians & Entertainment ✓

If a band or disc jockey is included in your reception plans, begin interviewing—or listening—when you book your reception site, about six months ahead.

☐ **Name(s)** _____   ☐ **Phone** _____

_____   _____

_____   _____

_____   _____

_____   _____

_____   _____

☐ Sound/repertoire _____

_____

_____

☐ Playing time _____
☐ Hours performing _____
☐ Arrival time _____
☐ Attire _____
☐ Special accommodations for equipment _____

_____

☐ Numbers/songs requested
1. _____
2. _____
3. _____
4. _____
5. _____
6. _____
7. _____
8. _____

9. _____
10. _____

☐ **Deposit $** _____ ☐ **Balance due $** _____

Notes

Estimates: ✓Photographer✓

Select your photographer about three months before the wedding. You may have one professional do your formal portraits (several weeks before) and another take candids on your wedding day.

☐ **Name** _____ ☐ **Phone** _____

	No. Neg.	How Many	Total
☐ **Portraits**			
☐ Engagement			
☐ Wedding			
☐ _____			
☐ **Candids**			
☐ Before the ceremony			
☐ During the ceremony			
☐ Reception			
☐ _____			
☐ Album(s)			
☐ **Extra sets**			
☐ Bride's parents			
☐ Groom's parents			
☐ Best man			
☐ Maid of honor			
☐ _____			
☐ _____			
☐ _____			
☐ _____			
☐ **Photographer's fee**			
☐ _____			
☐ _____			
☐ _____			

- ☐ **Total estimate $** _____
- ☐ **Actual cost $** _____
- ☐ **Deposit $** _____
- ☐ **Balance due $** _____
- ☐ **Arrival time** _____
- ☐ **Date photos will be ready** _____

Notes

Estimates:
✓ Photographer ✓

Select your photographer about three months before the wedding. You may have one professional do your formal portraits (several weeks before) and another take candids on your wedding day.

☐ **Name** _____ ☐ **Phone** _____

	No. Neg.	How Many	Total
☐ **Portraits**			
☐ Engagement			
☐ Wedding			
☐ _____			
☐ **Candids**			
☐ Before the ceremony			
☐ During the ceremony			
☐ Reception			
☐ _____			
☐ Album(s)			
☐ **Extra sets**			
☐ Bride's parents			
☐ Groom's parents			
☐ Best man			
☐ Maid of honor			
☐ _____			
☐ _____			
☐ _____			
☐ _____			
☐ **Photographer's fee**			
☐ _____			
☐ _____			
☐ _____			

- ☐ **Total estimate $** _____
- ☐ **Actual cost $** _____
- ☐ **Deposit $** _____
- ☐ **Balance due $** _____
- ☐ **Arrival time** _____
- ☐ **Date photos will be ready** _____

Notes

Estimates:
✓ Photographer ✓

Select your photographer about three months before the wedding. You may have one professional do your formal portraits (several weeks before) and another take candids on your wedding day.

☐ **Name** _____ ☐ **Phone** _____

	No. Neg.	How Many	Total
☐ **Portraits**			
☐ Engagement			
☐ Wedding			
☐ _____			
☐ **Candids**			
☐ Before the ceremony			
☐ During the ceremony			
☐ Reception			
☐ _____			
☐ Album(s)			
☐ **Extra sets**			
☐ Bride's parents			
☐ Groom's parents			
☐ Best man			
☐ Maid of honor			
☐ _____			
☐ _____			
☐ _____			
☐ _____			
☐ **Photographer's fee**			
☐ _____			
☐ _____			
☐ _____			

- ☐ **Total estimate $** _____
- ☐ **Actual cost $** _____
- ☐ **Deposit $** _____
- ☐ **Balance due $** _____
- ☐ **Arrival time** _____
- ☐ **Date photos will be ready** _____

Notes

3
For the Bride & Groom

Now you're going to focus on the needs of just you and your groom for a while—from the clothing to the gifts.

Begin with your WEDDING GOWN & ACCESSORIES. You may feel that you need an estimate worksheet as you did with the reception, but word has it that a bride usually falls in love with one dress, and then that's it: That's the _one_. Besides, you have more of a task just keeping up with your measurements, fittings, deposits, and color choices. Don't forget the camisole and lace stockings!

The GROOM'S ATTIRE is less of a long, complicated process of selection than yours may be, but nevertheless, there's a lot of information to keep at hand. Your fiancé needs to be measured before he orders his formal wear, and then he may need a few alterations. You both have a few decisions to make on style, too. Keep in mind that his attire will complement your dress, while his attendants' attire will nearly match his own. Still, this is an area where he should be able to play out his own tastes. Give him his checklist, then watch him go.

The checker for the ENGAGEMENT & WEDDING RINGS is loaded with options: Pick white gold, emeralds, clusters, or insets. That's not to say you're limited to what's on our list; your jeweler will be able to show you plenty of other rings. By the way, it's not a bad idea to refer to your ''Comparison Shopping & Contracts'' checklist from a previous section. And if you're not indebted to the family jeweler or enthralled by the gorgeous diamond solitaire in Zale's showcase, you might also pick up an estimate here and there before you buy. Before, or even after, you find out what's on the market, check off some boxes to get an idea of what you might like. Do it in pencil, and you can change your mind over and over again.

Your groom will probably make better use of the HONEYMOON checker, since tradition dictates that he arranges the trip. Of course, you should decide together whether it will be skiing in the Alps or swimming in Savannah. Then, he'll begin making reservations for transportation, lodging, meal plans, and so on. Later, you'll both be glad that you have a handy reference to take on your travels.

The GIFT REGISTRY is a walk through fantasyland; just how often can you actually pick and choose what you'd like to receive as a gift? It's not greedy at all; it's practical—even convenient for guests. Not only that, but you lessen the chances of duplication of gifts, since the store registry consultant updates records once a gift is selected.

You have a few different options: Pick a major department store for a variety of gifts, select a chain of stores for scattered guests, or choose a number of specialty shops for all kinds of prospects. Don't be afraid to list expensive gifts; some guests may want to go in on a present together for an especially nice offering. By the same token, don't leave out the inexpensive items: Those napkins are probably perfect for your niece's price range.

√ Wedding Gown √
& Accessories

This handy guide will help you keep your wedding attire coordinated so that the final result is perfect. If you begin shopping six months before your wedding, you'll have extra time to check out the selection and have your dress ready in time for formal portraits.

☐ **Gown**
   ☐ Shop _____   ☐ Phone _____
   ☐ Description _____
_____
   ☐ Measurements _____
_____
   ☐ Alterations/Fittings dates
       ☐ _____   ☐ _____   ☐ _____
   ☐ Cost $ _____   ☐ Deposit $ _____
   ☐ Balance due $_____   ☐ Pick-up date _____

☐ **Headpiece/veil**
   ☐ Shop _____   ☐ Phone _____
   ☐ Description _____
_____
   ☐ Measurements _____
_____
   ☐ Cost $ _____   ☐ Deposit $ _____
   ☐ Balance due $ _____   ☐ Pick-up date _____

☐ **Gloves**
   ☐ Shop _____   ☐ Phone _____
   ☐ Description _____
_____
   ☐ Cost $ _____   ☐ Pick-up date _____

☐ **Undergarments** (Color)
   ☐ Stockings _____ ☐ Slip _____

☐ Camisole _____ ☐ _____

☐ Shoes
   ☐ Shop _____   ☐ Phone _____
   ☐ Description _____

_____

   ☐ Size _____   ☐ Cost $ _____
   ☐ Pick-up date _____

Helpful Hints

- Remember that a gown doesn't arrive until about three months after you order it, and it takes about two more weeks for alterations.

- Choose your wedding dress first, then find the headpiece to match—unless you're wearing an heirloom veil; in that case shop for a dress to match its color.

- Arrange for someone to take your gown to a reliable dry cleaner after the ceremony. Some dry cleaners will specially treat and package a dress in an airtight box.

Notes

√Groom's Attire√

To the groom: Select your (and your attendants') attire three months before the wedding. Formal wear should be fitted and ordered at least a month before.

☐ **Shop** _____   ☐ **Phone** _____

☐ **Coat**   ☐ Size _____
  ☐ Description _____
_____

☐ **Vest/Cummerbund**   ☐ Size _____
  ☐ Description _____
_____

☐ **Trousers**   ☐ Size _____
  ☐ Description _____
_____

☐ **Shirt**   ☐ Size _____
  ☐ Description _____
_____

☐ **Tie**
  ☐ Description _____
☐ **Jewelry** (cufflinks, studs)
  ☐ Description _____
☐ **Shoes**   ☐ Size _____
  ☐ Description _____
☐ **Spats**   ☐ Size _____
  ☐ Description _____
☐ **Alterations/Fittings dates**
  ☐ _____   ☐ _____   ☐ _____
  ☐ Pick up _____   ☐ Return by _____
  ☐ Rental cost $ _____   ☐ Deposit $_____

Helpful Hints

- Your formal-wear specialist can rent shirts, shoes, spats, gloves, etc., but you may also purchase them elsewhere.

- The groom's formal wear usually matches his attendants' costumes, but you can always choose a slight variation to put yourself in the spotlight: shirt or tie of a different color, a white suit, a tailcoat, or different accessories.

- Make sure your formal wear fits: shirt collar should hug neck; shirt cuffs extend one-half inch or a little more beyond jacket sleeves; the trousers touch shoe tops.

- Pick up your suit two or three days ahead of time and try everything on immediately.

Notes

Engagement & Wedding Rings

If you and your groom choose to buy your rings together (which is advisable), fill out this checklist and take it along with you. But don't hesitate to change your mind; you might see something you like better.

Engagement

☐ **Metal**

    ☐ Gold: ☐ White   ☐ Yellow

               ☐ 14K   ☐ 18K   ☐ Other _____

    ☐ Platinum

☐ **Solitaire**

    ☐ Stone: ☐ Diamond   ☐ Sapphire

               ☐ Emerald   ☐ Ruby   ☐ Other ____

    ☐ Shape: ☐ Round (brilliant)

               ☐ Pearl (teardrop)

               ☐ Rectangular (emerald)

               ☐ Oval (marquise)

☐ **Band** (multistones)

    ☐ Diamonds   ☐ Emeralds   ☐ Sapphires

    ☐ Rubies   ☐ Other _____

☐ **Cluster**

    ☐ Diamonds   ☐ Emeralds   ☐ Sapphires

    ☐ Rubies   ☐ Other _____

☐ Description _____

☐ Size _____ ☐ Cost $ _____ ☐ Pick up _____

☐ Shop _____ ☐ Phone _____

Wedding (Indicate choices with ''B'' and ''G'' for bride and groom, if your rings differ.)

☐ **Metal**
   ☐ Gold: ☐ White   ☐ Yellow
              ☐ 14K   ☐ 18K   ☐ Other _____
   ☐ Platinum   ☐ Silver

☐ **Band**
   ☐ Singles   ☐ His and hers
   ☐ Inset stones _____
   ☐ Design _____

☐ **Other options** (See previous checklist; all are possibilities.) _____
_____

☐ Description _____
☐ Size _____ ☐ Cost $ _____ ☐ Pick up _____
☐ Shop _____ ☐ Phone _____

Helpful Hints

- Remove rings for heavy housework or gardening.

- Clean rings once a month with a commercial cleaner or with hot water and detergent.

Notes

√Honeymoon√

You and your groom should discuss your honeymoon preferences from Day One of the engagement. Begin making reservations six months before. This checklist should accompany you on your travels.

☐ Travel agent _____ ☐ Phone _____
☐ Address _____
☐ Agent rep. at travel site _____
☐ Address _____ ☐ Phone _____

Transportation

  Departure: ☐ Air   ☐ Rail   ☐ Ship   ☐ Bus
  ☐ Line name _____
    ☐ Take-off _____ ☐ Arrival _____
    ☐ Dates _____
  ☐ Ticket number _____
  ☐ Airport/Station _____
  ☐ Flight/Route number _____
  ☐ Class _____

  Return: ☐ Air   ☐ Rail   ☐ Ship   ☐ Bus
  ☐ Line name _____
    ☐ Take-off _____ ☐ Arrival _____
    ☐ Dates _____
  ☐ Ticket number _____
  ☐ Airport/Station _____
  ☐ Flight/Route number _____
  ☐ Class _____

  ☐ Confirmation date _____ ☐ Cost $_____
  ☐ Method of pay_____ ☐ Due _____

Lodging
- ☐ Hotel/motel _____
- ☐ Address _____
- ☐ Phone _____
- ☐ Reservations (800) _____
- ☐ Room description _____
- ☐ Check in _____ ☐ Time _____
- ☐ Check out _____ ☐ Time _____
- ☐ Daily rate $_____ ☐ Cost $_____
- ☐ Method of pay _____ ☐ Due _____

Meal Plan
- ☐ None ☐ One-Meal _____
- ☐ Two meals _____
- ☐ Three meals _____
- ☐ Other _____
- ☐ Cost $_____ ☐ Method of pay _____
- ☐ Due $ _____ ☐ Gratuity $_____

Helpful Hints

- Don't forget to take
- ☐ Proof of age, citizenship
- ☐ Marriage license
- ☐ Passport/visa
- ☐ List of credit card numbers
- ☐ List of traveler's check numbers
- ☐ List of luggage contents

Notes

✓*Gift Registry*✓

Make it easy on your guests, and get what you really need: Sign up at a wedding gift registry. Choose a wide variety of desirables—from inexpensive to expensive. You might choose a major department store registry for all your choices, or several specialty shops and chain stores.

☐ Formal dinnerware   ☐ Store _____

_____
_____
_____

☐ Crystal (or Glassware)   ☐ Store _____

_____
_____
_____

☐ Silver   ☐ Store _____

_____
_____
_____

☐ Linens   ☐ Store _____

_____
_____
_____

☐ Kitchen extras   ☐ Store _____

_____
_____
_____
_____

□ Bathroom extras   □ Store _____

_____
_____
_____
_____

□ Bedroom extras   □ Store _____

_____
_____
_____
_____

□ Appliances   □ Store _____

_____
_____
_____
_____

□ Home entertainment   □ Store _____

_____
_____
_____
_____

□ Others _____

_____
_____
_____
_____

Notes

4
Outfitting the Wedding Party

Your attendants go to a lot of trouble for you: They usually pay for their own attire, transportation, and lodging. They rush about, gathering measurements and fabric swatches, and pop up at every shower and party in your honor. And for what? Simply to accompany you while you and the groom take center stage. To toast you, hold your bouquet, and help you dress. To listen to you talk for hours on end about how you'll fix your hair to show off your headpiece.

Your attendants are chosen to be your right-hand people. You have to look at their situations objectively to really appreciate the effort. Because they deserve it, you should go out of your way to streamline their responsibilities. This section will help you see to all their needs and best serve *them*.

The BRIDESMAIDS' CLOTHING is much like yours; it matches the style of your dress and is often fitted and altered. In choosing their dresses, you'll have to go through a similar process as you did for yours. It's usually wise to take a maid or two along to help you choose since you'll want to consider what dresses look best on them. The dress color will be incorporated in the flowers and decorations, and you'll probably choose jewel tones for fall and winter, and pastels for spring and summer. All the maids usually wear the same color, unless you would like to differentiate your maid of honor with a deeper tone. You may even want to show her off with a dress of a different style or with an unusual bouquet. Record all that information on this checklist.

The MEN'S CLOTHING list will serve your groom best of all. He'll be pretty much in charge of coordinating the men's measurements and communicating to them the formal wear he wants them to wear. If you're lucky, every one lives in town and can conveniently be measured at the same shop. If attendants live out of town, however, they'll simply get measured in any shop in their respective cities. They'll send you the measurements, and then you'll just order the formal wear for them.

The men's attire may be identical to the groom's, except for maybe a variation to distinguish him: a shirt of a different color, tails, or a varying tie. The fathers don't have to wear the same suits as the attendants, but their suits should be similar.

The bridesmaids each carry a flower arrangement in a wedding; BOUQUETS are the most popular, but almost anything goes for the design—baskets, fans, muffs, candles—as long as it's similar to your own flower arrangement. You may decide that the maids will look best with flowers in their hair, but be sure the respective hairstyles lend themselves to the arrangements you choose.

All of the men—wedding party members and special guests—wear boutonnieres. The groom's flower complements the bride's bouquet and is different from those of the ushers and fathers, whose boutonnieres are the same. The corsages, for the mothers, grandmothers, and special guests, should feature a blossom or two from the bouquets.

The attendants will give you and the groom a gift, and in turn, you will give each of the attendants a gift to show your appreciation. GIFTS FOR THE WEDDING PARTY may be classic or original; we've prepared a list of ideas to help you choose. And don't forget your parents! They deserve the warmest of thanks. Say it with a gift, and then with a kiss.

✓ *Bridesmaids' Clothing* ✓

Your bridesmaids may be directly responsible for their own dresses, but chances are you'll have to coordinate sizes, fittings, and payment, not to mention color and style. We suggest, though, that you let your maid of honor take over this task. This checklist will help her.

Sizes

	Name	Dress	Bust/ Waist/ Hips	Glove	Shoe
☐	_____	____	____	____	____
☐	_____	____	____	____	____
☐	_____	____	____	____	____
☐	_____	____	____	____	____
☐	_____	____	____	____	____

Style

☐ Gown color   ☐ Maid of honor _____

                 ☐ Maids _____

☐ Gown style   ☐ MH _____

                 ☐ M(s) _____

☐ Headpiece color   ☐ MH _____

                 ☐ M(s) _____

☐ Headpiece style   ☐ MH _____

                 ☐ M(s) _____

☐ Fittings ☐ _____ ☐ _____

☐ Alterations   ☐ _____

   (each dress) ☐ _____

                ☐ _____

                ☐ _____

                ☐ _____

                ☐ _____

☐ Cost each:

☐ Dress $_____   ☐ Headpiece $ _____

Deposit (each maid)

    ☐ $ _____   ☐ $ _____

    ☐ $ _____   ☐ $ _____

    ☐ $ _____

Balance/due

    ☐ $ _____   ☐ $ _____

    ☐ $ _____   ☐ $ _____

    ☐ $ _____

☐ Final pick-up/delivery _____

☐ Shop _____   ☐ Phone _____

☐ Shoes ☐ Color _____   ☐ Style _____

☐ Pick-up _____   ☐ Cost $ _____

☐ Gloves ☐ Color _____   ☐ Style _____

☐ Pick-up _____   ☐ Cost $ _____

☐ Undergarments ☐ Stockings ☐ Camisoles

☐ Slips   ☐ Other _____

Helpful Hints

- The maid of honor dresses similarly to the maids in a deeper shade or slightly different dress style.

- Make three dress selections for your maids, and then allow them to make the final choice.

- Shoes for the attendants should be simple: Have them all dyed the same color, or simply ask them to choose a neutral shade.

- Buy gloves in the same place at the same time so they'll all match.

✓ Men's Clothing ✓

Traditionally, the groom, with the help of the best man, contacts groomsmen in advance for measurements. If they're from out of town, they'll need to go to a formal-wear shop elsewhere for sizing. For your convenience, the fathers' formal-wear details are included in this checklist, in case you'll be ordering all suits at the same shop or chain.

Sizes

Best man: ☐ Coat _____   ☐ Vest _____
  ☐ Trousers _____   ☐ Shirt _____
  ☐ Shoes _____   ☐ Other _____
Groomsman #1: ☐ Coat _____   ☐ Vest _____
  ☐ Trousers _____   ☐ Shirt _____
  ☐ Shoes _____   ☐ Other _____
Groomsman #2: ☐ Coat _____   ☐ Vest _____
  ☐ Trousers _____   ☐ Shirt _____
  ☐ Shoes _____   ☐ Other _____
Groomsman #3: ☐ Coat _____   ☐ Vest _____
  ☐ Trousers _____   ☐ Shirt _____
  ☐ Shoes _____   ☐ Other _____
Groomsman #4: ☐ Coat _____   ☐ Vest _____
  ☐ Trousers _____   ☐ Shirt _____
  ☐ Shoes _____   ☐ Other _____
Groomsman #5: ☐ Coat _____   ☐ Vest _____
  ☐ Trousers _____   ☐ Shirt _____
  ☐ Shoes _____   ☐ Other _____
Groom's father: ☐ Coat _____   ☐ Vest _____
  ☐ Trousers _____   ☐ Shirt _____
  ☐ Shoes _____   ☐ Other _____
Bride's father: ☐ Coat _____   ☐ Vest _____
  ☐ Trousers _____   ☐ Shirt _____
  ☐ Shoes _____   ☐ Other _____

Colors/styles (all usually same)
- ☐ Coats _____
- ☐ Vest/cummerbund _____
- ☐ Trousers _____
- ☐ Shirts _____
- ☐ Ties _____
- ☐ Jewelry _____
- ☐ Shoes _____
- ☐ Spats _____

Fittings
- ☐ Best man _____ ☐ Groomsman _____
- ☐ Groomsman _____ ☐ Groomsman _____
- ☐ Groomsman _____ ☐ Groomsman _____
- ☐ Father _____ ☐ Father _____

Cost each outfit $_____

Deposits/Paid:
- ☐ Best man ☐ Groomsman ☐ Groomsman
- ☐ Groomsman ☐ Groomsman ☐ Groomsman
- ☐ Father ☐ Father

Shop(s)/phone _____
_____
_____

Final pick-up/delivery _____

Notes

The bride's bouquet should be the most prominent in style among the other women's flowers, but all should be similar in formality (*not* informal daisies on the bridesmaids and formal orchids on the bride). Flower colors and arrangements will coordinate with the dresses. The maid of honor's arrangement may differ slightly from the bridesmaids'.

Bride

☐ Style: ☐ Cascade   ☐ Nosegay
   ☐ Long stems   ☐ Basket   ☐ Single
   ☐ Prayer book   ☐ Other _____
☐ Flowers/Color:
   ☐ Orchids _____   ☐ Daisies _____
   ☐ Camellias _____   ☐ Gardenias _____
   ☐ Carnations _____   ☐ Lilies _____
   ☐ Roses _____   ☐ Sweet peas _____
   ☐ Stephanotis _____   ☐ _____
   ☐ _____   ☐ _____
☐ Greenery: ☐ Ivy   ☐ Ferns
   ☐ _____   ☐ _____
☐ Fillers: ☐ Baby's breath   ☐ Queen Anne's lace
   ☐ Candytuft ☐ _____
☐ Hair blossoms: _____

Maid of honor

☐ Style: ☐ Cascade   ☐ Nosegay   ☐ Basket
   ☐ Fan   ☐ Muff   ☐ Other _____
☐ Flowers/Color:
   ☐ Orchids _____   ☐ Daisies _____
   ☐ Camellias _____   ☐ Gardenias _____
   ☐ Carnations _____   ☐ Lilies _____
   ☐ Roses _____   ☐ Sweet peas _____

- ☐ Stephanotis _____ ☐ _____
- ☐ _____ ☐ _____
- ☐ Greenery: ☐ Ivy ☐ Ferns
- ☐ _____ ☐ _____
- ☐ Fillers: ☐ Baby's breath ☐ Queen Anne's lace
  - ☐ Candytuft ☐ _____
- ☐ Hair blossoms: _____

Maids

- ☐ Style: ☐ Cascade ☐ Nosegay ☐ Basket
  - ☐ Fan ☐ Muff ☐ Other _____
- ☐ Flowers/Color:
  - ☐ Orchids _____ ☐ Daisies _____
  - ☐ Camellias _____ ☐ Gardenias _____
  - ☐ Carnations _____ ☐ Lilies _____
  - ☐ Roses _____ ☐ Sweet peas _____
  - ☐ Stephanotis _____ ☐ _____
  - ☐ _____ ☐ _____
- ☐ Greenery: ☐ Ivy ☐ Ferns
  - ☐ _____ ☐ _____
- ☐ Fillers: ☐ Baby's breath ☐ Queen Anne's lace
  - ☐ Candytuft ☐ _____
- ☐ Hair blossoms: _____

Helpful Hints

- A bouquet is a matter of personal preference; a bride may also wear flowers on her dress, on a belt around the waist, on a sash draped from the shoulder to waist, or on a muff around the wrist.

Notes

Flowers:
✓Corsages & Boutonnieres✓

Groom
☐ Rose   ☐ Carnation   ☐ Stephanotis
☐ Lily of the valley   ☐ Other _____

Best man
☐ Rose   ☐ Carnation   ☐ Stephanotis
☐ Lily of the valley   ☐ Other _____

Groomsmen (Number _____)
☐ Rose   ☐ Carnation   ☐ Stephanotis
☐ Lily of the valley   ☐ Other _____

Fathers (Number _____)
☐ Rose   ☐ Carnation   ☐ Stephanotis
☐ Lily of the valley   ☐ Other _____

Special guests (Number _____)
☐ Rose   ☐ Carnation   ☐ Stephanotis
☐ Lily of the valley   ☐ Other _____

Bride's Mother (Dress color _____)
☐ Roses   ☐ Carnations   ☐ Orchids
☐ Daisies   ☐ Other _____
☐ Baby's breath   ☐ Fern   ☐ Ivy

Groom's Mother (Dress color _____)
☐ Roses   ☐ Carnations   ☐ Orchids
☐ Daisies   ☐ Other _____
☐ Baby's breath   ☐ Fern   ☐ Ivy

Grandmothers (Number _____)
☐ Roses   ☐ Carnations   ☐ Orchids
☐ Daisies   ☐ Other _____
☐ Baby's breath   ☐ Fern   ☐ Ivy

Special guests (Number _____)

☐ Roses ☐ Carnations ☐ Orchids
☐ Daisies ☐ Other _____
☐ Baby's breath ☐ Fern ☐ Ivy

Helpful Hints

- It's nice to remember the musicians, soloists, and people performing special duties (serving punch, keeping the guest book) with a boutonniere or corsage (they'll all be the same). Don't forget sisters, brothers, or elderly relatives that you may wish to honor.

- The mothers' corsages are similar for easy identification, but you'll want to check with them before you order. Remember, each mother's dress should coordinate with their flowers!

- The groom's boutonniere complements the bride's bouquet, and is usually different from those of the groomsmen and fathers.

Notes

Gifts for the Wedding Party

A gift for your attendants, as well as for both sets of parents is a way of saying "thank-you." Choose some of the classics, below, or think of your own original ideas. Many times, brides choose the same gift for all bridesmaids, but you and your groom may want to pick something a little special for your honor attendants, or maybe something different for all. The all-time favorite is to choose a piece of jewelry that attendants may wear in the wedding, with their initials or your wedding date monogrammed on it. Present your gifts at the bridesmaids' luncheon, bachelor's party, or at the rehearsal dinner.

☐ **Gift Ideas**
☐ Bridesmaids monogrammed:
    ☐ Bracelet   ☐ Pin   ☐ Charm
    ☐ Pendant ☐ Pen/pencil set

    ☐ Personalized stationery   ☐ Compact
    ☐ Comb/brush set   ☐ Pearl earrings
    ☐ Silk scarf   ☐ Manicure kit
    ☐ Framed wedding photo

☐ Groomsmen monogrammed:
    ☐ Money clip   ☐ Key ring   ☐ Cuff links
    ☐ Bar jigger ☐ Gold/silver lighter ☐ Belt buckle
    ☐ Tie tack ☐ Stickpin ☐ Pewter mug

    ☐ Silk tie   ☐ Wallet   ☐ Manicure set
    ☐ Pen/pencil set

☐ Parents:
    ☐ Framed wedding photo   ☐ Framed invitation
    ☐ Crystal decanter/paperweight with wedding date inscription   ☐ Laminated certificate of appreciation   ☐ Theater/concert tickets

☐ **Chosen Gifts**

☐ Maid of honor _____
   ☐ Store _____ ☐ Pick-up _____

☐ Bridesmaids _____
   ☐ Store _____ ☐ Pick-up _____

☐ Best man _____
   ☐ Store _____ ☐ Pick-up _____

☐ Groomsmen _____
   ☐ Store _____ ☐ Pick-up _____

☐ Parents _____
   ☐ Store _____ ☐ Pick-up _____

☐ Others _____
   ☐ Store _____ ☐ Pick-up _____

Helpful Hints

- You might also remember special people who were here when you needed them: the neighbors who served as chauffeurs, the college friend who kept the guest book, or the aunt who lent a hand with meal preparation.

Notes

5
Tying Up the Ends

It's winding up now, but you still have a million things to do to finish plans for the wedding. A number of lists here will put those next-to-last steps in order.

Get those invitations taken care of first. When you visit the engraver or stationer, take the checker along to record specifics. A few of the usual options are included here, but the stationer will show you his entire selection, if you wish. Ask for a chance to proofread a sample before the order is printed. *Always* check spellings and the old-fashioned wording against your list.

Fill out the guest list in the INVITATION/RSVP checker, and check off affirmations once they start rolling in.

With all that you have to do, the REHEARSAL DINNER shouldn't take too much of your time, especially since someone else usually hosts it for you. You will, however, be expected to help decide a few of the details, such as where and when to hold it and who to invite. Let the host know a month or so before, then confirm it two to three weeks before the wedding.

How will you get to the ceremony and reception? Give some thought to your TRANSPORTATION and hire professional drivers, or get a few neighbors and relatives to chauffeur you and the wedding party. There's a checker here to direct the drivers to the sites, and a passenger list, too. Make several copies and fill one out for each driver; be sure to save a copy of each for your records.

You know nothing about applying for the MARRIAGE LICENSE? A call to the city/county clerk will clear up any mysteries. Your checker here pretty much tells you what you need to bring along. Don't forget to schedule your blood tests first, since you need to have the results before you can apply. Before you make any LEGAL NAME CHANGE decisions, read over our rundown of options. We tell you the pros and cons, and then the decision is up to you. When you have decided what it will be, there's a checklist telling you how to spread the news. This is a big deal, and you want to spread the good news to the world! What better way than with a NEWSPAPER ANNOUNCEMENT? Follow our step-by-step guide, but call the appropriate person at the publication(s) in which you would like the announcement to appear: There are usually specifics to follow for each newspaper.

In order to efficiently put together THE BAR for your reception, you need to organize in advance. The checker here is multipurpose, of sorts. The only information actually provided is the list of liquors, mixers, and equipment you may need. The rest *you* fill in. This checklist is perfect for recording the inventory before and after the party, to help you arrive at a cost.

Look at your CANDIDS LIST and you'll see a multitude of photo possibilities for your photographer. Because we've only included the most obvious of choices, you might want to add your own ideas. At the end of the checker, list the people who you won't want your photographer to miss.

What with all the talk about RECEIVING LINES and SEATING PLANS, many etiquette or planning books assume that you know exactly what to do. Well, maybe you do, and maybe you don't. In any case, our guide will fill you in on the order of the receiving line and variations, as well as what to say when you're greeting guests. On the back side of the checker are a couple of suggestions for reception seating, but feel free to mix and match guests as you please.

√Invitations√

Visit your jeweler, department store, stationer, or bridal salon to order invitations at least three months before the wedding, and take this checklist along with you to help (ask to see several selections). Then, mail in time for the invitations to arrive three weeks—and not less than two weeks—before the wedding.

Style
☐ Print
   ☐ Engraved (more expensive)   ☐ Printed
☐ Color
   ☐ White (formal)   ☐ Ivory (formal)
   ☐ Parchment   ☐ Shiny metallic
   ☐ Other _____
☐ Size
   ☐ 4½″ x 5¾″ (popular)   ☐ 5½″ x 7½″
   ☐ Other _____
☐ Type
   ☐ Script (romantic)   ☐ Roman (dignified)
   ☐ Other _____
☐ Enclosure cards
   ☐ Reception   ☐ Ceremony   ☐ RSVP
   ☐ At-home   ☐ Pew   ☐ Other _____
☐ Additional items
   ☐ Announcements   ☐ Napkins
   ☐ Thank-you notes   ☐ Matchbooks
   ☐ Other _____
☐ Number invitations _____ ☐ Cost per $ _____
☐ Cost extras $ _____
☐ Total cost $ _____

Chosen wording
  1. _____

2. _____
3. _____
4. _____
5. _____
6. _____
7. _____
8. _____
9. _____
10. _____

Proofreading corrections

_____
_____
_____

Helpful Hints

- The first line should note who is sponsoring or hosting the wedding, but not necessarily paying for it.

- Make sure that you are able to proofread a sample before the order is printed up.

- Get a headstart on addressing envelopes by having the stationer send them to you early.

- Request extra invitations for your families as keepsakes, and order spare envelopes in case you make a mistake.

Notes

✓Rehearsal Dinner✓

Traditionally, the groom's parents host the rehearsal party, but anyone may have the honor. If it's convenient, schedule it two or three nights before the wedding; that way, everyone can celebrate royally and have time to rest before the big event. But if need be (important people are out of town?), have your rehearsal dinner the night before; just call it off early. The host should confirm the dinner about two weeks before the wedding. (See also the ''Rehearsal'' checklist, in Section 6.)

☐ **Date** _____ ☐ **Time** _____
☐ **Place** _____
☐ **Confirmed** _____ ☐ **Deposit** _____

☐ **Menu**
_____
_____
_____
_____
_____

☐ **Guest list:**

1. _____
2. _____
3. _____
4. _____
5. _____
6. _____
7. _____
8. _____
9. _____
10. _____
11. _____
12. _____

13. _____
14. _____
15. _____
16. _____
17. _____
18. _____
19. _____
20. _____
21. _____
22. _____
23. _____
24. _____
25. _____
26. _____
27. _____
28. _____
29. _____
30. _____

Helpful Hints

- Invite the wedding party, their spouses, your immediate families, the officiant and spouse, and probably the musicians, soloists. You *might* want to invite out-of-town relatives and friends.

- Wear something nice to the rehearsal, especially if you'll be in a church or fine restaurant.

Notes

Transportation

Perhaps you'll hire limousine drivers to take you to the ceremony and reception, or maybe friends and relatives will offer to chauffeur you and the wedding party. Here's the usual order, but remember that it's your option.

☐ **To the ceremony**
   Car 1: Groom and best man
   Car 2: Bridesmaids
   Car 3: Mother of the bride and friend, relative, or maid
            of honor
   Car 4: Bride and her father

☐ **To the reception**
   Car 1: Bride and groom
   Car 2: Bride's parents
   Car 3: Best man and maid of honor
   Car 4: Bridesmaids

Give all of your drivers, hired or otherwise, a copy of the list below. Keep one for your own records, too.

☐ **Driver's name** _____
☐ Address _____ ☐ Phone _____

☐ **Passengers**
☐ Name _____ ☐ Phone _____
☐ Address _____
_____

☐ Name _____ ☐ Phone _____
☐ Address _____
_____

☐ Name _____ ☐ Phone _____
☐ Address _____
_____

☐ Name _____ ☐ Phone _____
☐ Address _____
_____

☐ **Pick-up address** _____
☐ Arrival time _____ ☐ Directions _____
_____
_____

☐ **Ceremony site** _____
☐ Address _____ ☐ Phone _____
☐ Directions _____
_____
_____

☐ **Reception site** _____
☐ Address _____ ☐ Phone _____
☐ Directions _____
_____
_____

Notes

✓ *Marriage License* ✓

Two or three weeks before the wedding, you and the groom should apply for your marriage license at the city clerk's office. But first, schedule a blood test and physical examination, since you'll need the results to take with you (most states require this procedure). Check with your county clerk's office to inquire about "the age of consent" (marriage without parents' approval), as it may apply, as well as other requirements in your state.

- ☐ **Blood tests/examinations**
    - ☐ Bride
        - ☐ Dr._____
        - ☐ Phone _____ ☐ Appt. _____
        - ☐ Results due _____
    - ☐ Groom
        - ☐ Dr. _____
        - ☐ Phone _____ ☐ Appt. _____
        - ☐ Results due _____
- ☐ **License**
    - ☐ Date to apply _____ ☐ Time _____
    - ☐ City clerk office _____ ☐ Phone _____
    - ☐ Address _____
    - ☐ Fee $_____
- ☐ Bring:
    - ☐ Identification (driver's license)
    - ☐ Proof of age (birth certificate, baptismal record, adoption record, passport, naturalization certificate)
    - ☐ Citizenship papers (if it applies)
    - ☐ Blood tests results
    - ☐ Doctor's certificates
    - ☐ Proof of divorce (if it applies)
- ☐ **Waiting period for license** _____
- ☐ **License validity dates** _____

Helpful Hints

- State requirements for blood tests vary. Some may be for syphilis or may also include rubella and sickle-cell anemia.

- Don't forget: Some states have a waiting period of one to five days before you actually receive license after application.

- A few states have a waiting period *after* issuing the license before it's valid.

- Only certified photocopies of age verification documents are accepted.

- The groom usually pays the license fee.

- Two witnesses, usually your honor attendants, sign your marriage license, either at the rehearsal dinner or on the wedding day.

Notes

√ *Legal Name Change* √

It's a sign of the times: More and more women think before deciding what their married names will be. Here are your options, plus some pros and cons.

☐ **His name.** It's the traditional, most popular choice. Pro: You and your husband will do what is socially more accepted and understood. Con: You may have already developed a career name for yourself, and a name change could lose credibility for you.

☐ **Your name.** You'll be Cynthia Hall and he'll be Richard Lee, just as you've always been. Pro: You won't have to change legal documents. Con: Many people will assume that you're Mrs. Lee.

☐ **Combine names.** "Cynthia Hall Lee," may be hyphenated. Pro: You'll be honoring both names, and clients or co-workers will make the connection. Con: You'll still have to change document titles, and the hyphen may get lost on computerized forms.

☐ **Both combine names.** Cynthia and Richard Hall-Lee. Pro: No one gives up anything. Con: Lots of red tape for both you, not to mention your children.

Spreading the name news

☐ At-home cards (with invitation)
Mr. and Mrs. Richard Lee
or Cynthia Hall and Richard Lee

☐ Enclosure Cards (with invitation)
Cynthia Hall and Richard Lee wish to announce that both will be retaining their present names for all legal and social purposes.

☐ Thank-you notes	When you're sending out notes after the wedding, sign your preferred name.
☐ Business cards	Cynthia Hall announces she has adopted the surname Lee.
☐ Newspaper announcement	Make sure your name preference is printed correctly when the announcement is published.

Offices to Contact

☐ County Clerk (voter's registration)   ☐ Motor Vehicles Bureau (driver's license, car registration)

☐ Social Security   ☐ Post Office   ☐ Insurance

☐ Bank   ☐ Credit cards   ☐ Stocks, bonds

☐ Wills   ☐ Leases   ☐ School records

☐ Employment records   ☐ Property titles

☐ Passport ☐ Other _____

☐ _____   ☐ _____

☐ _____   ☐ _____

Notes

✓ *Newspaper* ✓
Announcements

Contact the lifestyle editors of you and your groom's hometown newspapers two months or so in advance for a wedding announcement. Policies for publications differ, but here's a standard procedure to guide you.

First

☐ Meet a publication's deadline. Some require a standard form to be submitted a week or two before the wedding.

☐ Type essential information on one side of plain, white, 8½ × 11 inch paper. Then include:

Upper right corner

☐ Name

☐ Address

☐ Telephone number (a relative, perhaps, for wedding verification)

Upper left corner

☐ Date of announcement

☐ Include in your announcement those details permitted by the publication.

☐ Wedding date, time

☐ Ceremony site

☐ All parents' names

☐ Officiant

☐ Your dress description

☐ Your bouquet description

☐ Attendants' names, relations, residences

☐ Bridesmaids' dresses, bouquets (descriptions)

☐ Reception location

☐ Couple's education, professional background

☐ All grandparents' names

☐ Honeymoon plans

Publications

- ☐ _____ ☐ Phone _____
- ☐ Editor _____ ☐ Deadline _____
- ☐ Mailing address _____

- ☐ _____ ☐ Phone _____
- ☐ Editor _____ ☐ Deadline _____
- ☐ Mailing address _____

- ☐ _____ ☐ Phone _____
- ☐ Editor _____ ☐ Deadline _____
- ☐ Mailing address _____

Notes

√ The Bar √

Organizing the reception bar is *some* task, especially if you plan a big party with an open bar. This list will either help an amateur keep up with what liquor, mixes, and equipment is needed. Or, it will serve as a measure of how much you owe the banquet manager after the reception.

☐ **Liquor** (Brand? Number? Cost? etc.)
   ☐ Champagne _____
   ☐ Red wine _____
   ☐ Rosé wine _____
   ☐ White wine _____
   ☐ Bourbon _____
   ☐ Rum _____
   ☐ Gin _____
   ☐ Scotch _____
   ☐ Vodka _____
   ☐ _____
   ☐ _____

☐ **Mixers**
   ☐ Cola _____
   ☐ Soda _____
   ☐ Ginger ale _____
   ☐ Tonic _____
   ☐ Seltzer _____
   ☐ Collins mix _____
   ☐ Bloody Mary mix _____
   ☐ Grapefruit juice _____
   ☐ Lime juice _____
   ☐ Orange juice _____
   ☐ Tomato juice _____

- ☐ _____
- ☐ _____

☐ Ingredients
- ☐ Ice _____
- ☐ Limes _____
- ☐ Lemons _____
- ☐ Olives _____
- ☐ Maraschino cherries _____
- ☐ _____

☐ Equipment
- ☐ Openers (bottle, can) _____ ☐ Spoons _____
- ☐ Knives _____ ☐ Corkscrews _____
- ☐ Swizzle sticks _____ ☐ Shakers _____
- ☐ Blender _____ ☐ Cocktail napkins _____
- ☐ Glasses: ☐ Tumblers _____ ☐ Wine _____
  - ☐ Champagne _____ ☐ _____
  - ☐ _____ ☐ _____
- ☐ Champagne served at what time _____
- ☐ Open bar hours _____

Notes

√ Candids List √

These are some of the classic, obvious photo possibilities. Add some of your own ideas or strike the ones you don't want. Then give this list to your photographer. (Keep a copy for yourself, too.)

☐ **Before the ceremony**
- ☐ Bride dressing   ☐ Bride with mother
- ☐ Bride with both parents   ☐ Bride with attendants
- ☐ Bride and attendants receiving flowers
- ☐ Attendants inspecting bride's dress, flowers, hair
- ☐ Attendants leaving for ceremony
- ☐ Bride and father leaving for ceremony

_____

_____

- ☐ Groom dressing   ☐ Groom with parents
- ☐ Groom with best man   ☐ Groom with attendants
- ☐ Groom, attendants receiving boutonnieres
- ☐ Groom leaving for ceremony

_____

☐ **At the ceremony**
- ☐ Arriving guests   ☐ solists and organist
- ☐ Ushers escorting guests   ☐ Groom arriving
- ☐ Bride, father arriving   ☐ Processional
- ☐ Groom meeting bride at altar   ☐ Altar lineup
- ☐ Exchanging vows, rings   ☐ The kiss
- ☐ Recession   ☐ Couple leaving for reception

_____

_____

☐ **Posed shots**
- ☐ Bride and groom   ☐ Couple with wedding party
- ☐ Couple with child attendants   ☐ Couple with officiant   ☐ Couple with both sets of parents

☐ Couple with honor attendants   ☐ Couple with both families

_____

_____

☐ **At the reception**
   ☐ Couple arriving   ☐ The receiving line
   ☐ Toasts to couple   ☐ The tables
   ☐ Cutting cake   ☐ Feeding each other cake
   ☐ Couple dancing   ☐ Bride, father dancing
   ☐ Groom, his mother dancing   ☐ Other couples
   ☐ The musicians   ☐ Bride throwing bouquet
   ☐ Groom throwing garter   ☐ Bride changing
   ☐ Groom changing
   ☐ Couple saying good-bye to parents
   ☐ Couple leaving   ☐ Guests throwing rice
   ☐ Couple getting into car
   ☐ Guests waving good-bye

_____

_____

_____

_____

_____

_____

_____

Notes

√Receiving Line √
& Seating Plan √

The wedding party will look to you for instructions on the receiving line. This list spells out the traditional order. Each person in line introduces himself or herself to the guest, and in turn introduces the guest to the next party member in line.

1. Bride's mother
2. Groom's mother
3. Bride
4. Groom
5. Maid of honor
6. Bridesmaids

Helpful Hints

- If you and the groom host, you head the receiving line (if you prefer to).

- If your parents are divorced and your stepmother is hosting with your father, she stands at the head of the line.

- If your mother is deceased, your father may stand at the head of the line with a female relative. Of course, you may organize the receiving line any other way you wish.

- Keep conversation short, but say something special to everyone. A good example: "Mrs. Everson, thank you for the spice rack; it was delivered yesterday. You've met my new husband, Steve, haven't you?" The groom might say: "Yes, we met at Sarah's recital, didn't we? It's nice to see you again. Mrs. Everson, this is Lisa's good friend, Gwen Riddle (the maid of honor). Gwen, this is Sarah's mother. Have you met before?"

Notes

The most important thing to see to when you're arranging the reception seating plan is that the newlyweds sit at the head of the table in a prominent location (facing the guests). The possibilities are endless, but here are the most popular and practical plans.

☐ Option 1:

Bride and groom's table

3	1	2	4
5			6
6			5
5			6

1. Bride 2. Groom 3. Best man 4. Maid of honor
5. Bridesmaids 6. Groomsmen

☐ Option 2:

Honor Table

1	2	3	4	5	6

1. Groom's mother 2. Groom's father 3. Bride
4. Groom 5. Bride's mother 6. Bride's father

Helpful Hints

- You might arrange a parents' table where the parents, officiant and spouse, and grandparents sit.

- Have two tables for parents if they are divorced.

- Always alternate males and females.

Notes

6
Getting Ready

As you approach the final days of your single life, you'll be organizing and scheduling the wedding. Although there should be others to look after the time planning for you (such as your attendants and the best man), you—and the wedding party—could use some cues about what happens when.

The REHEARSAL is a step-by-step rundown of what everyone needs to practice on the rehearsal dinner night. It might help to make several copies to distribute; add any extra notes that may need to be announced—one more time.

The SCHEDULES will be a tremendous help for the major members of your party. There's a timetable for each person for the wedding day. You can help by filling in some of the obvious times on the schedules before you distribute them.

Let's start with you, the BRIDE and your schedule. Your timetable, like everyone else's, is fairly streamlined; we included the major events, your next move, and instructions—throughout the event. You probably won't want to carry your checker around with you during the festivities, but a review of it before the ceremony may give you an extra feeling of calm. Knowing that the MAID OF HONOR is following her own checker will also be a comfort. (Feel free to renumber the sequence, if your wedding is not quite as we describe.)

Your GROOM has a schedule, too, although he'll depend a great deal on the best man to be his stopwatch and personal valet. The BEST MAN, then, has his work cut out for him; and as you can see, his schedule is quite lengthy. He's master of ceremonies and advisor to the ushers too.

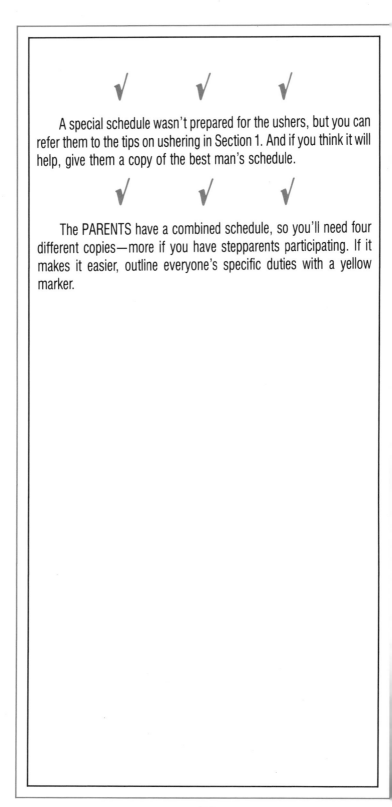

A special schedule wasn't prepared for the ushers, but you can refer them to the tips on ushering in Section 1. And if you think it will help, give them a copy of the best man's schedule.

The PARENTS have a combined schedule, so you'll need four different copies—more if you have stepparents participating. If it makes it easier, outline everyone's specific duties with a yellow marker.

√Rehearsal√

Three days to one day before the wedding, before the rehearsal dinner begins, you'll meet with the wedding party for practice at the ceremony site. Go through everything without actually saying the vows. These step-by-step instructions show you how.

☐ Give ushers escort instructions. (See ''The Wedding Party.'')

☐ Give head usher or best man list of guests with special seating.

☐ Have soloists or musicians run through music for ceremony.

☐ Walk through the procession; begin on the left foot, and keep a distance of four pews between each bridesmaid.

☐ Have everyone stand in appropriate places.

☐ Practice passing bouquets. When you reach the altar, the maid of honor will hand the next attendant her bouquet and take yours.

☐ Listen to your officiant explain your responses and when to pass the rings.

☐ Retrieve your bouquet in the right hand before you take off on the groom's right arm. Your maid of honor promptly takes her bouquet back from the nearby bridesmaid.

☐ Instruct ushers as to how to empty church; perhaps they'll bow out each row or allow guests to leave without assistance.

☐ Assign certain ushers to arrange pew ribbons, unroll and roll white carpet in the aisle, collect prayer books, and direct guests to the reception.

☐ Fill everyone in on the last-minute details: Double-check wedding transportation; explain what will happen in the receiving line; tell the ushers to be at the wedding site an hour early.

Helpful Hints

- Make fake bouquets with gift-ribbon bows so you can practice passing them.

- If you're writing your own ceremony, give everyone at the rehearsal a copy so they'll know what happens when.

- It might be wise to wear your wedding shoes to the rehearsal; better to trip down the aisle tonight than tomorrow!

Notes

Schedule:  √ *Bride* √

Your wedding schedule may vary, but this is an ideal time frame. Once the day arrives, leave the worry and supervision to the consultants and professionals; you've earned this day for yourself.

Time

☐ _____ Flowers arrive at your home or at the ceremony site.

☐ _____ Begin dressing in time to arrive at the ceremony 5 minutes beforehand.

☐ _____ Have home candids made.

☐ _____ Give the groom's ring to the maid of honor.

☐ _____ Leave with your father for the ceremony.

☐ _____ Arrive at the ceremony site; assemble in the foyer.

☐ _____ Begin the procession with your father, following maids.

☐ _____ Meet your groom at the altar, take his left arm, and pass your bouquet to the maid of honor.

☐ _____ Officiant begins ceremony, you say vows, exchange rings. Groom or maid of honor lifts your veil; you and the groom kiss.

☐ _____ Take bouquet back in right hand, let maid of honor arrange your veil, turn to face guests, take your groom's arm.

☐ _____ You and the groom take off for the reception site, photos, the pastor's quarters, or a receiving line in the foyer.

(Order for reception is optional. Number yours accordingly.)

☐ _____ Participate in receiving line.

☐ _____ Champagne is served.

☐ _____ Toasting begins.

☐ _____ Dinner or refreshments are announced, about an hour after reception begins.

☐ _____ You and the groom cut cake. Pick up a knife decorated with ribbons (perhaps flowers?), and the groom covers his right hand over yours. Cut into bottom layer and share first slice.

☐ _____ You and groom dance first to favorite song.

☐ _____ Dance with your father, then best man, then groom's father.

☐ _____ Everyone dances.

☐ _____ (Last half hour) Throw bouquet; then groom removes garter from your leg and throws it.

☐ _____ Leave reception to change into going-away clothes.

☐ _____ Tell parents good-bye.

☐ _____ Leave for honeymoon under shower of rice.

Notes

Schedule:
✓ Groom ✓

Here's a typical rundown of your big day. Look to your best man for any assistance—and prompting—you might need.

Time

☐ _____ Your boutonniere is delivered to your home, or at the ceremony site.

☐ _____ Begin dressing in time to arrive at the ceremony site twenty minutes beforehand.

☐ _____ Give the best man the bride's ring, officiant's fee, and any keys, tickets, or money to hold until honeymoon time.

☐ _____ Leave for the church with the best man.

☐ _____ (20 minutes before) Arrive at ceremony site; assemble in vestibule.

☐ _____ (Ceremony time) Take your place at the officiant's left.

☐ _____ Meet your bride at the altar. She'll take your left arm.

☐ _____ Officiant begins ceremony, you say vows, exchange rings. Lift bride's veil, if maid of honor doesn't, then kiss her.

☐ _____ Turn to face guests; bride takes your right arm.

☐ _____ You and bride take off for the reception site, photos, the pastor's quarters, or a receiving line in the foyer.

(Order for reception is optional. Number yours accordingly.)

☐ _____ Participate in receiving line.

☐ _____ Champagne is served.

☐ _____ Toasting begins: best man first, then you thank him. Follow with a toast to your bride, your parents, and/or her parents.

- [ ] ____ Dinner or refreshments are announced, about an hour after reception begins.
- [ ] ____ You and bride cut cake. Cover your right hand over bride's right hand as she cuts into bottom layer. Share first slice.
- [ ] ____ Dance the first song with bride.
- [ ] ____ Dance with the bride's mother, then the maid of honor, then your mother.
- [ ] ____ Everyone dances.
- [ ] ____ (Last half hour) After the bride throws bouquet, remove garter from her leg; throw it to the single men.
- [ ] ____ Leave reception to change into going-away clothes.
- [ ] ____ Tell parents good-bye.
- [ ] ____ Leave for honeymoon under shower of rice.

Notes

Schedule:
√ *Best Man* √

You're in charge of the groomsmen and/or ushers, and the groom. You're also the master of ceremonies, so you have an important job.

Time

☐ _____ Get dressed and go to the groom's home.

☐ _____ Take the bride's ring, officiant's fee, and any keys, tickets, or money to hold until honeymoon time.

☐ _____ See that you and the groom arrive at the ceremony site about 20 minutes early. (The other groomsmen should be there about an hour to 45 minutes early.)

☐ _____ When you and the groom arrive, give the officiant his fee. Assemble in the vestibule.

☐ _____ See that the ushers are following seating instructions, or if they have any questions.

☐ _____ (Ceremony time) Take your place at the front of the church, at the left and a little behind the groom.

☐ _____ Give the groom the ring when the officiant asks for it during the ceremony.

☐ _____ Follow the bride and groom with the maid of honor on your right arm in the recession.

☐ _____ Head for photos with the rest of the wedding party, but also help supervise the ushers as they direct guests to the reception. Drive the couple to the reception site.

(Order for reception is optional. Number yours accordingly.)

☐ _____ Mingle with guests while others are in the receiving line.

- ☐ ____ When champagne is served, you propose first toast to the bride and groom.
- ☐ ____ Dinner or refreshments are announced.
- ☐ ____ You (or bandleader) announce the cutting of the cake.
- ☐ ____ You (or bandleader) announce first dance.
- ☐ ____ Dance with the bride, the maids, and the mother.
- ☐ ____ (Last half hour) You (or bandleader) announces the throwing of the bouquet and garter.
- ☐ ____ Help the groom undress and get into going-away clothes.
- ☐ ____ Help groom get organized for the honeymoon (tickets, money, keys, luggage).
- ☐ ____ Drive couple to hotel, airport, station, or new home.

Notes

Schedule:
√ *Maid of Honor* √

Look after the bride, look after the bridesmaids, remember your cues, and you'll do a great job.

Time

☐ ____ Get dressed either at your home or the bride's home.

☐ ____ Help the bride get dressed.

☐ ____ Take the groom's ring and slip it on your fore-finger until the ceremony.

☐ ____ Leave for the ceremony, with the maids or the bride's mother, in time to arrive 15 minutes before the ceremony.

☐ ____ Arrive at the ceremony; assemble in the foyer.

☐ ____ (Ceremony time) When the groom and grooms-men have assembled at the front of the church, the processional music gets louder and the guests stand up; the maids step into the processional, one at a time. You follow them and precede the bride.

☐ ____ Take your place at the front of the church and turn to see the bride reach the altar.

☐ ____ Hand your bouquet to a nearby maid and take the bride's bouquet.

☐ ____ Give bride the groom's ring when the officiant asks for it.

☐ ____ Lift the bride's veil (optional) before the couple's kiss.

☐ ____ Give the bride back her bouquet, then arrange her train before she takes off for the recessional.

☐ ____ Retrieve your bouquet, then take the best

man's arm to follow the bride and groom down the aisle.

☐ _____ Either head for photos with the wedding party, or ride to the reception with the maids.

(Order for reception is optional. Number yours accordingly.)

☐ _____ Participate in the receiving line.

☐ _____ Champagne is served.

☐ _____ Toasting begins.

☐ _____ Dinner or refreshments are announced.

☐ _____ The couple cuts the cake.

☐ _____ Dancing begins. Eventually, you'll dance with all the male attendants.

☐ _____ (Last half hour) Help assemble the single women for the throwing of the bouquet.

☐ _____ Help the bride undress and get ready to leave.

Notes

Schedule: Parents

You've already achieved the best of roles by producing the children who star in this wedding. But don't be so fast to bow out! Your schedules:

Time

☐ _____ Groom's parents dress at home.

☐ _____ Bride's mother dresses, poses for pictures, and leaves with maid of honor or friend in time to arrive 15 minutes before ceremony.

☐ _____ Bride's father dresses, poses for pictures, and leaves with bride in time to arrive five minutes before the ceremony.

☐ _____ (15 minutes before) Before any musical solos begin, groom's parents are seated in front pew, right side of main aisle. Bride's mother is then seated in front pew, left side.

☐ _____ After groom and groomsmen assemble at front of church, the bride's mother stands to signal that everyone stand.

☐ _____ After maids have stepped down the aisle, bride's father escorts bride to altar on his left arm.

☐ _____ When the bride reaches groom at the altar, father slips into his pew.

☐ _____ When the officiant addresses the giving-away question, the bride's parents answer, ''We do.'' Or, the bride's father may answer before he sits down.

☐ _____ When the ceremony is over, the ushers return to escort the mothers out of the church. Fathers or husbands follow behind them.

☐ ____ The mothers usually participate in receiving line; the fathers may or may not.

☐ ____ Champagne is served.

☐ ____ Toasting begins. Fathers may offer a toast after the best man and groom.

☐ ____ Dinner or refreshments are announced.

☐ ____ The couple cuts the cake.

☐ ____ After the bride and groom dance, the bride's father dances with the bride, while the bride's mother dances with the groom. Eventually, the groom's father dances with the bride, the groom's mother with her son.

☐ ____ The bride throws the bouquet; the groom throws the garter.

☐ ____ The couple leaves party to change; the parents leave to tell them good-bye.

☐ ____ The couple leaves for the honeymoon.

☐ ____ The bride's father signals the musicians to stop playing. The bride's parents thank everyone for coming and stay until the last guest leaves.

Notes

✓ *Invitations & RSVP List* ✓

Send your invitations so that they arrive two to three weeks before the wedding. This way, you'll have time to receive RSVPs and perhaps invite additional people who didn't make the first round of preferred guests.

1. Name(s) _____ No. _____
Address _____ RSVP ☐

2. Name(s) _____ No. _____
Address _____ RSVP ☐

3. Name(s) _____ No. _____
Address _____ RSVP ☐

4. Name(s) _____ No. _____
Address _____ RSVP ☐

5. Name(s) _____ No. _____
Address _____ RSVP ☐

6. Name(s) _____ No. _____
Address _____ RSVP ☐

7. Name(s) _____ No. _____
Address _____ RSVP ☐

8. Name(s) _____ No. _____
Address _____ RSVP ☐

9. Name(s) _____ No. _____
Address _____ RSVP ☐

10. Name(s) _____ No. _____
Address _____ RSVP ☐

11. Name(s) _____ No. _____
Address _____ RSVP ☐

12. Name(s) _____ No. _____
Address _____ RSVP ☐

13. Name(s) _____ No. _____
Address _____ RSVP ☐

14. Name(s) _____ No. ____
Address _____ RSVP ☐
15. Name(s) _____ No. ____
Address _____ RSVP ☐
16. Name(s) _____ No. ____
Address _____ RSVP ☐
17. Name(s) _____ No. ____
Address _____ RSVP ☐
18. Name(s) _____ No. ____
Address _____ RSVP ☐
19. Name(s) _____ No. ____
Address _____ RSVP ☐
20. Name(s) _____ No. ____
Address _____ RSVP ☐
21. Name(s) _____ No. ____
Address _____ RSVP ☐
22. Name(s) _____ No. ____
Address _____ RSVP ☐
23. Name(s) _____ No. ____
Address _____ RSVP ☐
24. Name(s) _____ No. ____
Address _____ RSVP ☐
25. Name(s) _____ No. ____
Address _____ RSVP ☐
26. Name(s) _____ No. ____
Address _____ RSVP ☐
27. Name(s) _____ No. ____
Address _____ RSVP ☐
28. Name(s) _____ No. ____
Address _____ RSVP ☐
29. Name(s) _____ No. ____
Address _____ RSVP ☐

30. Name(s) _____ No. ____
Address _____ RSVP ☐

31. Name(s) _____ No. ____
Address _____ RSVP ☐

32. Name(s) _____ No. ____
Address _____ RSVP ☐

33. Name(s) _____ No. ____
Address _____ RSVP ☐

34. Name(s) _____ No. ____
Address _____ RSVP ☐

35. Name(s) _____ No. ____
Address _____ RSVP ☐

36. Name(s) _____ No. ____
Address _____ RSVP ☐

37. Name(s) _____ No. ____
Address _____ RSVP ☐

38. Name(s) _____ No. ____
Address _____ RSVP ☐

39. Name(s) _____ No. ____
Address _____ RSVP ☐

40. Name(s) _____ No. ____
Address _____ RSVP ☐

41. Name(s) _____ No. ____
Address _____ RSVP ☐

42. Name(s) _____ No. ____
Address _____ RSVP ☐

43. Name(s) _____ No. ____
Address _____ RSVP ☐.

44. Name(s) _____ No. ____
Address _____ RSVP ☐

45. Name(s) _____	No. ___
Address _____	RSVP ☐
46. Name(s) _____	No. ___
Address _____	RSVP ☐
47. Name(s) _____	No. ___
Address _____	RSVP ☐
48. Name(s) _____	No. ___
Address _____	RSVP ☐
49. Name(s) _____	No. ___
Address _____	RSVP ☐
50. Name(s) _____	No. ___
Address _____	RSVP ☐
51. Name(s) _____	No. ___
Address _____	RSVP ☐
52. Name(s) _____	No. ___
Address _____	RSVP ☐
53. Name(s) _____	No. ___
Address _____	RSVP ☐
54. Name(s) _____	No. ___
Address _____	RSVP ☐
55. Name(s) _____	No. ___
Address _____	RSVP ☐
56. Name(s) _____	No. ___
Address _____	RSVP ☐
57. Name(s) _____	No. ___
Address _____	RSVP ☐
58. Name(s) _____	No. ___
Address _____	RSVP ☐
59. Name(s) _____	No. ___
Address _____	RSVP ☐
60. Name(s) _____	No. ___
Address _____	RSVP ☐

61. Name(s) _____	No. ____
Address _____	RSVP ☐
62. Name(s) _____	No. ____
Address _____	RSVP ☐
63. Name(s) _____	No. ____
Address _____	RSVP ☐
64. Name(s) _____	No. ____
Address _____	RSVP ☐
65. Name(s) _____	No. ____
Address _____	RSVP ☐
66. Name(s) _____	No. ____
Address _____	RSVP ☐
67. Name(s) _____	No. ____
Address _____	RSVP ☐
68. Name(s) _____	No. ____
Address _____	RSVP ☐
69. Name(s) _____	No. ____
Address _____	RSVP ☐
70. Name(s) _____	No. ____
Address _____	RSVP ☐
71. Name(s) _____	No. ____
Address _____	RSVP ☐
72. Name(s) _____	No. ____
Address _____	RSVP ☐
73. Name(s) _____	No. ____
Address _____	RSVP ☐
74. Name(s) _____	No. ____
Address _____	RSVP ☐
75. Name(s) _____	No. ____
Address _____	RSVP ☐

76. Name(s) _____	No. ____
Address _____	RSVP ☐
77. Name(s) _____	No. ____
Address _____	RSVP ☐
78. Name(s) _____	No. ____
Address _____	RSVP ☐
79. Name(s) _____	No. ____
Address _____	RSVP ☐
80. Name(s) _____	No. ____
Address _____	RSVP ☐
81. Name(s) _____	No. ____
Address _____	RSVP ☐
82. Name(s) _____	No. ____
Address _____	RSVP ☐
83. Name(s) _____	No. ____
Address _____	RSVP ☐
84. Name(s) _____	No. ____
Address _____	RSVP ☐
85. Name(s) _____	No. ____
Address _____	RSVP ☐
86. Name(s) _____	No. ____
Address _____	RSVP ☐
87. Name(s) _____	No. ____
Address _____	RSVP ☐
88. Name(s) _____	No. ____
Address _____	RSVP ☐
89. Name(s) _____	No. ____
Address _____	RSVP ☐
90. Name(s) _____	No. ____
Address _____	RSVP ☐
91. Name(s) _____	No. ____
Address _____	RSVP ☐

92. Name(s) _____ No. ____
Address _____ RSVP ☐
93. Name(s) _____ No. ____
Address _____ RSVP ☐
94. Name(s) _____ No. ____
Address _____ RSVP ☐
95. Name(s) _____ No. ____
Address _____ RSVP ☐
96. Name(s) _____ No. ____
Address _____ RSVP ☐
97. Name(s) _____ No. ____
Address _____ RSVP ☐
98. Name(s) _____ No. ____
Address _____ RSVP ☐
99. Name(s) _____ No. ____
Address _____ RSVP ☐
100. Name(s) _____ No. ____
Address _____ RSVP ☐
101. Name(s) _____ No. ____
Address _____ RSVP ☐
102. Name(s) _____ No. ____
Address _____ RSVP ☐
103. Name(s) _____ No. ____
Address _____ RSVP ☐
104. Name(s) _____ No. ____
Address _____ RSVP ☐
105. Name(s) _____ No. ____
Address _____ RSVP ☐
106. Name(s) _____ No. ____
Address _____ RSVP ☐

107. Name(s) _____	No. ____	
Address _____	RSVP ☐	
108. Name(s) _____	No. ____	
Address _____	RSVP ☐	
109. Name(s) _____	No. ____	
Address _____	RSVP ☐	
110. Name(s) _____	No. ____	
Address _____	RSVP ☐	
111. Name(s) _____	No. ____	
Address _____	RSVP ☐	
112. Name(s) _____	No. ____	
Address _____	RSVP ☐	
113. Name(s) _____	No. ____	
Address _____	RSVP ☐	
114. Name(s) _____	No. ____	
Address _____	RSVP ☐	
115. Name(s) _____	No. ____	
Address _____	RSVP ☐	
116. Name(s) _____	No. ____	
Address _____	RSVP ☐	
117. Name(s) _____	No. ____	
Address _____	RSVP ☐	
118. Name(s) _____	No. ____	
Address _____	RSVP ☐	
119. Name(s) _____	No. ____	
Address _____	RSVP ☐	
120. Name(s) _____	No. ____	
Address _____	RSVP ☐	

√Gift List√

Gifts will begin to arrive as soon as you announce your wedding date. Keep track of what you receive and your thank-you replies with these handy checklists.

1. Name/Address _____
Gift _____ Thank-you sent ☐
2. Name/Address _____
Gift _____ Thank-you sent ☐
3. Name/Address _____
Gift _____ Thank-you sent ☐
4. Name/Address _____
Gift _____ Thank-you sent ☐
5. Name/Address _____
Gift _____ Thank-you sent ☐
6. Name/Address _____
Gift _____ Thank-you sent ☐
7. Name/Address _____
Gift _____ Thank-you sent ☐
8. Name/Address _____
Gift _____ Thank-you sent ☐
9. Name/Address _____
Gift _____ Thank-you sent ☐
10. Name/Address _____
Gift _____ Thank-you sent ☐
11. Name/Address _____
Gift _____ Thank-you sent ☐
12. Name/Address _____
Gift _____ Thank-you sent ☐
13. Name/Address _____
Gift _____ Thank-you sent ☐

14. Name/Address _____
Gift _____ Thank-you sent ☐
15. Name/Address _____
Gift _____ Thank-you sent ☐
16. Name/Address _____
Gift _____ Thank-you sent ☐
17. Name/Address _____
Gift _____ Thank-you sent ☐
18. Name/Address _____
Gift _____ Thank-you sent ☐
19. Name/Address _____
Gift _____ Thank-you sent ☐
20. Name/Address _____
Gift _____ Thank-you sent ☐
21. Name/Address _____
Gift _____ Thank-you sent ☐
22. Name/Address _____
Gift _____ Thank-you sent ☐
23. Name/Address _____
Gift _____ Thank-you sent ☐
24. Name/Address _____
Gift _____ Thank-you sent ☐
25. Name/Address _____
Gift _____ Thank-you sent ☐
26. Name/Address _____
Gift _____ Thank-you sent ☐
27. Name/Address _____
Gift _____ Thank-you sent ☐
28. Name/Address _____
Gift _____ Thank-you sent ☐

29. Name/Address _____
Gift _____ Thank-you sent ☐
30. Name/Address _____
Gift _____ Thank-you sent ☐
31. Name/Address _____
Gift _____ Thank-you sent ☐
32. Name/Address _____
Gift _____ Thank-you sent ☐
33. Name/Address _____
Gift _____ Thank-you sent ☐
34. Name/Address _____
Gift _____ Thank-you sent ☐
35. Name/Address _____
Gift _____ Thank-you sent ☐
36. Name/Address _____
Gift _____ Thank-you sent ☐
37. Name/Address _____
Gift _____ Thank-you sent ☐
38. Name/Address _____
Gift _____ Thank-you sent ☐
39. Name/Address _____
Gift _____ Thank-you sent ☐
40. Name/Address _____
Gift _____ Thank-you sent ☐
41. Name/Address _____
Gift _____ Thank-you sent ☐
42. Name/Address _____
Gift _____ Thank-you sent ☐
43. Name/Address _____
Gift _____ Thank-you sent ☐

44. Name/Address _____
Gift _____ Thank-you sent ☐
45. Name/Address _____
Gift _____ Thank-you sent ☐
46. Name/Address _____
Gift _____ Thank-you sent ☐
47. Name/Address _____
Gift _____ Thank-you sent ☐
48. Name/Address _____
Gift _____ Thank-you sent ☐
49. Name/Address _____
Gift _____ Thank-you sent ☐
50. Name/Address _____
Gift _____ Thank-you sent ☐
51. Name/Address _____
Gift _____ Thank-you sent ☐
52. Name/Address _____
Gift _____ Thank-you sent ☐
53. Name/Address _____
Gift _____ Thank-you sent ☐
54. Name/Address _____
Gift _____ Thank-you sent ☐
55. Name/Address _____
Gift _____ Thank-you sent ☐
56. Name/Address _____
Gift _____ Thank-you sent ☐
57. Name/Address _____
Gift _____ Thank-you sent ☐
58. Name/Address _____
Gift _____ Thank-you sent ☐

59. Name/Address _____
Gift _____ Thank-you sent ☐
60. Name/Address _____
Gift _____ Thank-you sent ☐
61. Name/Address _____
Gift _____ Thank-you sent ☐
62. Name/Address _____
Gift _____ Thank-you sent ☐
63. Name/Address _____
Gift _____ Thank-you sent ☐
64. Name/Address _____
Gift _____ Thank-you sent ☐
65. Name/Address _____
Gift _____ Thank-you sent ☐
66. Name/Address _____
Gift _____ Thank-you sent ☐
67. Name/Address _____
Gift _____ Thank-you sent ☐
68. Name/Address _____
Gift _____ Thank-you sent ☐
69. Name/Address _____
Gift _____ Thank-you sent ☐
70. Name/Address _____
Gift _____ Thank-you sent ☐
71. Name/Address _____
Gift _____ Thank-you sent ☐
72. Name/Address _____
Gift _____ Thank-you sent ☐
73. Name/Address _____
Gift _____ Thank-you sent ☐

74. Name/Address _____
Gift _____ Thank-you sent ☐
75. Name/Address _____
Gift _____ Thank-you sent ☐
76. Name/Address _____
Gift _____ Thank-you sent ☐
77. Name/Address _____
Gift _____ Thank-you sent ☐
78. Name/Address _____
Gift _____ Thank-you sent ☐
79. Name/Address _____
Gift _____ Thank-you sent ☐
80. Name/Address _____
Gift _____ Thank-you sent ☐
81. Name/Address _____
Gift _____ Thank-you sent ☐
82. Name/Address _____
Gift _____ Thank-you sent ☐
83. Name/Address _____
Gift _____ Thank-you sent ☐
84. Name/Address _____
Gift _____ Thank-you sent ☐
85. Name/Address _____
Gift _____ Thank-you sent ☐
86. Name/Address _____
Gift _____ Thank-you sent ☐
87. Name/Address _____
Gift _____ Thank-you sent ☐
88. Name/Address _____
Gift _____ Thank-you sent ☐
89. Name/Address _____
Gift _____ Thank-you sent ☐

90. Name/Address _____

Gift _____ Thank-you sent ☐

91. Name/Address _____

Gift _____ Thank-you sent ☐

92. Name/Address _____

Gift _____ Thank-you sent ☐

93. Name/Address _____

Gift _____ Thank-you sent ☐

94. Name/Address _____

Gift _____ Thank-you sent ☐

95. Name/Address _____

Gift _____ Thank-you sent ☐

96. Name/Address _____

Gift _____ Thank-you sent ☐

97. Name/Address _____

Gift _____ Thank-you sent ☐

98. Name/Address _____

Gift _____ Thank-you sent ☐

99. Name/Address _____

Gift _____ Thank-you sent ☐

100. Name/Address _____

Gift _____ Thank-you sent ☐

101. Name/Address _____

Gift _____ Thank-you sent ☐

102. Name/Address _____

Gift _____ Thank-you sent ☐

103. Name/Address _____

Gift _____ Thank-you sent ☐

104. Name/Address _____

Gift _____ Thank-you sent ☐

105. Name/Address _____
Gift _____ Thank-you sent ☐
106. Name/Address _____
Gift _____ Thank-you sent ☐
107. Name/Address _____
Gift _____ Thank-you sent ☐
108. Name/Address _____
Gift _____ Thank-you sent ☐
109. Name/Address _____
Gift _____ Thank-you sent ☐
110. Name/Address _____
Gift _____ Thank-you sent ☐
111. Name/Address _____
Gift _____ Thank-you sent ☐
112. Name/Address _____
Gift _____ Thank-you sent ☐
113. Name/Address _____
Gift _____ Thank-you sent ☐
114. Name/Address _____
Gift _____ Thank-you sent ☐
115. Name/Address _____
Gift _____ Thank-you sent ☐
116. Name/Address _____
Gift _____ Thank-you sent ☐
117. Name/Address _____
Gift _____ Thank-you sent ☐
118. Name/Address _____
Gift _____ Thank-you sent ☐
119. Name/Address _____
Gift _____ Thank-you sent ☐
120. Name/Address _____
Gift _____ Thank-you sent ☐

Index

Notes

Notes

Notes